My Little Valentine
(The story of a mother and daughter's lost love)

KelLee Parr

Copyright © 2016 KelLee Parr
All rights reserved.
Printed in the U.S.A.

Dedication

This story is dedicated to my beloved mother and grandmothers. It is also dedicated to all the heartbroken young women who gave their babies up for adoption. Never give up hope.

Acknowledgments

This is the true story of my mother and grandmother's journey to find one another. The story is factual and based on my personal experiences, information shared by family members, and hundreds of letters between mother and daughter. Some of the details and storyline are fictional, as I filled in the blanks as best I remembered or expected they happened. As I tell this story, I am sad to say both my beloved mother and grandmother have passed on. A few names have been changed to provide anonymity for certain characters and their families.

This book would not have happened without the encouragement and support of my friend, coworker, editor and proofreader, Margaret Heisserer. Thank you for pressing me to tell my mother and grandmother's story.

Thank you also to my friend, Rachelle Mengarelli, for your wonderful input, as you know my family and me as well as anyone. My mother appreciated your friendship and all you did for her as well. Amazing how fast thirty years fly by, but so happy to have had you as a friend along the journey.

Also, I would like to thank Patrice Scott for your editing and great feedback. As someone that had never heard the story, you helped make the story flow. I so appreciate your research about The Willows to be able to tell that part of the story more accurately.

To my graphic designer, Trista Bieberle, thank you for the wonderful design of the cover. It is exactly what I had envisioned.

Thank you to Laurel Elliot, dvb New York, for the use of the image of your beautiful necklace for the cover.

Finally, to my sisters, Jane and Janice, thanks for your support and help with remembering all the details from our mother's story and being the best sisters ever. Thanks to my nephew, Bo, and niece, EJ, for making Granny feel so special and for your help with my website and providing photos. Thanks to my cousins Mick and Skip for their help with information about the Kellers, and to Robert for your friendship and support.

The image of The Willows is from the December 24, 1908 issue of the *Kansas City Star*.

The following were very helpful resources:

> Articles from *St. Marys Star*, St. Marys, Kansas, "A Different Kind of Love Story" August 27, 1991 by Dorothy Hoobler; "Lynn and Emma Keller Observe Their 66th Anniversary" March 1980 by their daughters; "Lindsay Keller Will Celebrate 100th Birthday" December 11, 1990.
>
> Book by Geneva Keller Fairbanks, *Precious "Keller" Memories*
>
> Book by Thomas M Perry, Jr., *Bahner History*
>
> *Biography of the Barron and Connected Families* compiled by A.M. Barron

For readers interested in knowing more about Leona and Wanda's story, check out photos and additional information at my website: www.mylittlevalentinebook.com

I would also love to hear from others who have a connection to The Willows. I was totally amazed to find out the role The Willows had in so many lives from 1905 to 1969 and how Kansas City was the adoption hub of America. Hopefully through my website, people can share and learn from others about their backgrounds and connect with lost family members.

My Little Valentine

Chapter 1

♡♡

Summer 1991

"Where have you been? I've been dying for you to get home. It came! It came! The letter, it came!" Ellen screamed as she emerged from the back room of her condo. This letter could be the answer to the secret Ellen and I had been sharing for months.

My confidant was my fiftyish, next door neighbor in the condominium complex where I lived. We lived in the Barcelona building between Madrid and Seville though we never quite got the feeling we were living in Spain while actually living in Topeka, Kansas. It was our common interest in flowers and gardening that sparked our friendship.

Ellen moved in across the hall in the fall of 1990. She had a flair for life and had that gravelly Marlena Dietrich voice from years of smoking. She was as thin as a rail and had difficulty breathing at times. I understood from her determined spirit why Ellen, even with emphysema caused from years of puffing on cigarettes, would move to a second floor condo with no elevator. The lady just wanted to prove she could do it.

Many a night after work, Ellen would sit out on her balcony, smoke a cigarette, and twist macramé cord to make some new device to hang more plants. More often than not, the only way I knew Ellen was even out on the balcony was by the cigarette smoke billowing up over the jungle of entangled flowers. If not doing something with her flowers, she often would have a book in hand, transported to a far off place. But then again, the book could be one of her smutty romance novels with a bare chested "Fabio" look alike on the front cover.

At least a couple nights a week after work, I would join Ellen on her little balcony that looked out over the courtyard of our complex. We would sit on the colorful flowered cushions on her white wicker chairs and chat the early evening hours away. There was usually a new remodeling project she was working on in her condo, and it was fun to watch the progress. We would share stories about our families, and she told me all about her upbringing in rural Kansas, which was not that far from where my maternal grandpa was born. Ellen told me how she loved to travel and would often take off on vacation to one of the destinations she had read about in one of her travel books.

Another amazing Ellen fact was that even with the breathing problems that had been developing over the past few years, she was starting to take ballroom dancing lessons and would go bowling at least once a week. "Nothing will stop me from enjoying life," she said.

She told me about the new boyfriend she had met ballroom dancing, and knowing she would make me blush said with her sly grin on her face, "You know there is no way I would ever marry again, but I sure am enjoying the sex." We both laughed and I felt like she was reading a line from one of her smutty novels.

My family and what was going on in my life and at school were always of interest to Ellen. She was a natural born listener that made you feel you could share anything and know it went no further. She enjoyed meeting my family and especially loved my dad. The fact my dad raved about her beautiful flower garden didn't hurt.

On evenings it was too cold to sit outside, Ellen would knock on my door and we would sit in my living room and catch up on the day's events. She loved sitting in the antique oak rocking chair with a bright red pillow that had been my grandfather's and hearing the story about how I had asked for his rocking chair when he passed away. It was the one thing of his I wanted.

I remembered seeing Grandpa Parr sitting on the porch in his rocker as I pedaled up the hill on my Schwinn stingray bike with the cool silver banana seat to visit Grandma and Grandpa. Blessed as a kid to live only a quarter mile from two of the best grandparents in the world, Grandpa would wave to me as I turned into the driveway. He would never get up because he, like Ellen, had emphysema from smoking those filterless, self-rolled cigarettes. Though I never remembered seeing him smoke, my dad said Grandpa gave off more smoke than our old potbellied stove in the woodshop.

Grandma Parr was a short, stout, tough little German lady. Her maiden name was Immenschuh—now that's German! She was about as wide as she was tall. Grandpa was a thin-as-a-rail Englishman. Talk about Jack Sprat and his wife. Grandpa was quiet and easy going. Grandma was a little opinionated and stubborn. In fact, she didn't speak to her own sister for almost 30 years over a fight about their parent's coal oil light that they both had wanted and her sister got. Though amicable, one would never say she and my mother, Wanda, were close. Grandma adored my dad and she had a way of making my mother feel that maybe she just wasn't quite good enough for my dad.

I was spoiled rotten by both of my grandparents because I was the youngest grandchild. During the summer as a kid, I would spend countless hours with them. We would play cards and caroms, or I would help Grandma make her wonderful molasses cookies. I would ride to town with her to get groceries in her old gray '54 Ford. She was so short she had to look through the steering wheel to see the road. I am sure many a driver thought that car was driving itself.

I showed Ellen a treasure that was my grandma's. When I was eight years old, my grandma had shown me a hiding place in the attic of her clothes closet. There was a little wooden ladder in the closet to get to the door to the attic. One time when I was visiting, she told me she wanted to show me something, and she climbed up the ladder and brought down a box just a little larger than a shoebox.

Grandma told me to sit on the bed. I was excited to find out what the secret was in the box. Grandma laid the box on her bed next to me and opened it displaying a red velvet box inside. She carefully lifted it out of the cardboard box and sat it on my lap. It was a writing desk that her father had brought over from Germany. She pulled out a key on a piece of green yarn and unlocked the lock on the side of the box. The little lid at the top of the box opened upward and inside there were three writing pens and an inkwell. The larger flat lid then opened down and inside were several keepsakes, including Grandma's ribbons from the Kansas State Fair for her quilts. One final surprise was when Grandma pulled the section with the pens and inkwell out and there was a secret compartment. It was just the right size to keep rings or valuable coins. Grandma told me that one day this box was to be mine. She wanted me to have it.

I told Ellen that after my grandparents had passed and the family all gathered to go through their belongings, each grandkid got to choose one belonging. I chose Grandpa's rocker. After everyone had picked I said to my dad and uncle, "Grandma said I could have her red velvet writing box."

They both just looked at me and said they had no idea what I was talking about. I said follow me and marched into my grandma's bedroom. I climbed the ladder and pushed back the attic door and the only thing up there was the little box. I grabbed it and handed it to my dad who was holding me so I didn't fall off the ladder. Once off the ladder I took the box and showed them all the writing desk. My uncle said, "Well I'll be. Never knew that even existed. I guess it is yours for sure." The fact I was the only one that Grandma ever told about her treasure made it even more special to me.

Another bit of family trivia Ellen was especially enamored with was my mother's adoption in the mid-1920s. It struck a chord because Ellen told me she was adopted as an infant. We talked at length about how being adopted can affect a person. For Ellen, it was the root of her insecurity and abandonment issues. She helped me understand a lot more about my mother and the many ways being adopted had made Mother be the person she was.

Ellen related to me and my family on so many levels. We spent many hours sharing life's little moments, what went on with her work with the crazies at the state department, and which of my third graders had made some great "kids say the darnedest things" comment that day. So it was no wonder I shared my secret with Ellen. For months Ellen was the only person in the world I had told the secret, which led to our excitement about the letter. We were both aware how this letter could change things. But in actuality, this secret was not mine at all. It was way older than me. In fact, it was more than 60 years old and I was just possibly going to be the one to expose it.

Chapter 2

♡

February 1925

It was a cold winter night and she lay in her bed in the pitch-dark room she had come to know as "home" the past three months. She heard the rhythmic breathing of the other two girls sleeping in their beds, also imprisoned in the room. The blinds on the windows were always closed except when one of the girls was daring enough to peek out against orders and see the lights of the streetcar in the street passing by. The girls never got to leave the mausoleum-like building except once a day to walk the worn path that encircled the garden. She felt claustrophobic in her room, even with a little dresser, writing desk and mirror beside her bed. She missed her simple room she shared with her sister back home. Each night was the same. Silent sobs, longing for her mother's loving arms.

She pulled the quilt up over her shivering shoulders and curled her legs up under her in the fetal position. She tried to sleep. Every time she closed her eyes she thought of her parents and how much she missed them. She envisioned their small farm back in Kansas. She could smell the fresh hay stored in the red barn. She heard the sounds of the chickens clucking and cows mooing. She saw herself fishing and hunting with her papa and could almost feel the warm sun on her face. She could picture her family sitting around their kitchen table, laughing at the latest story her little brother was telling about his run-in with the skunk down at the creek.

The sterile smell of the room brought her thoughts back to her current situation and why she was in this cold dark place. Her body ached. She heard sobs from another girl in the room, apparently not asleep either and feeling as lonely and sad as she was. Does that girl's body hurt as bad as hers does? As a tear slowly rolled down her cheek, she finally drifted off to sleep not knowing what tomorrow would bring and if she lived, the burden of the secret she would have for the rest of the days of her life.

Chapter 3

July 1991

Teaching allowed me to spend a couple weeks in the summer visiting my sister, Jane, in Ponte Vedra Beach, Florida. I absolutely loved spending time with her and soaking up sun on the beach. The summer of 1991 was no different though it was the first time I was going on vacation reluctantly. This secret that only Ellen and I shared made me want to stay close to home. Whenever either Ellen or I made plans to be gone for any length of time, we automatically collected the other's letters, bills, newspapers, and magazines.

For days Ellen had teased me about stalking the mailbox like Ralphie in *A Christmas Story,* waiting for the Little Orphan Annie Ovaltine Secret Decoder Ring. But now it was time for me to go on vacation. My hopes of the anticipated letter were still high but nothing had arrived. With suitcase in hand as I headed off to surf, sand and sun, Ellen was more than anxious to volunteer to get my mail.

My Florida vacations were always full of adventure but also plenty of relaxation. Shortly after I arrived, it was the day of the birth of our country. We headed to St. Augustine with friends to watch the fireworks at the old fort Castillo de San Marcos. Our group found a spot for our blanket on the grass amongst the other hundreds of onlookers. We had some time to snack on our picnic items while we awaited the sun to disappear and the big fireworks show to begin over the water of the Mantanzas Bay. Jane sensed something was off when I seemed distracted and a little quiet. She asked if there was anything bothering me. I brushed it off as exhaustion from school and needing to unwind, though I was wondering if my anticipated letter had arrived back home.

Several days later at the beach, Jane and I were reclining in beach chairs, our toes in the sand, enjoying the sound of the waves hitting the beach and our bodies soaking up the sun. We began reminiscing about our parents and our days back on the farm. I was bursting to tell my sister about what was making me so anxious. At last I couldn't hold it in. I had to spill my guts.

Chapter 4

It all started the previous year. In the fall of 1990, I began my first year of teaching with my very own classroom of kids. When I graduated from Kansas State University in 1978 with an animal science degree, I never would have believed I would be teaching third grade one day. After living and working for three years in Guatemala as an agricultural missionary and then four years in Kansas working as the Elk County Extension Agricultural and 4-H Agent, I decided at the age of thirty to go back to college to get my teaching degree. My thought was to teach middle school social studies. I was assigned to do my student teaching under a fantastic teacher named Mr. Manley who taught a third/fourth grade combination classroom and found I really enjoyed that age group. Upon graduation, I fortunately found a job teaching third grade.

My first year was flying by—March and spring break came very quickly. Wouldn't you know, spring break arrived and I had a bad cold. I hadn't been sick the entire school year. Though I had no real plans, my spring break started by just staying home and sneezing and coughing the week away. By the end of the week I was feeling somewhat better and needed to get out of my condo.

While working on lessons for my third graders' social studies units throughout the year, one of the student outcomes I needed to teach was about our state and the city of Topeka in particular. The history of Topeka was really something I had very little knowledge about so I needed to research to prepare lessons for my students that I would teach after spring break.

A fellow teacher suggested I check out the Kansas Historical Society located in downtown Topeka across from the state capitol building. (There was no such thing as the Internet or Google searches at my disposal then.) So I decided to use one of my last spring break days and check it out. I always loved history and that was part of the reason I considered teaching social studies at the middle school level.

The lady at the information desk of the historical society happily gave me a tour of the building. The state historical society was fascinating. She shared that President William Howard Taft laid the cornerstone of the limestone building in 1911. In 1984, a new museum was built as the old building had become outgrown. They still archived all the old records and it was filled with history. I loved all the tidbits of information about Topeka and Kansas. Taking lots of notes and grabbing pamphlets along the way, this was giving some great direction for my lessons that my students would find interesting and fun to learn.

My tour guide led me to the room where all the state records were archived. It was a cavernous room that echoed and felt like one of those libraries where you were expecting a grumpy librarian to shush you if you uttered a peep. The room had large, heavy wooden tables and chairs for people to sit and look through the massive ledger-like books on the shelves. These books contained state history and census information dating back to Kansas statehood in 1861. The census information was also stored on microfiche.

Four or five people were scattered around the room looking through books. In the center of the room were maybe a half dozen or so machines on small individual tables each with a wooden chair. These machines were to view the historical data on the microfiche. A few people were using the machines and my guide said they were usually looking for ancestors and tracing their family history. Something clicked in my head. "My mother, what if?"

Chapter 5

My mother had given my sisters, Jane and Janice, and me each a copy of her adoption papers the previous year. It was those adoption papers that came to mind when I saw the people searching for their family histories. Could this be a means to help my mother find information about her birth parents?

Wanda June Keller Parr was adopted as an infant by Lindsay and Emma Keller. She was officially adopted on April 11, 1925.

Wanda was an extremely accomplished and talented woman. She was an outstanding seamstress, excelled at sports—even playing softball on a women's league team in Topeka before she was married—a fantastic cook, great carpenter, did leathercraft, was a meticulous housekeeper, and maintained beautiful landscaping around the farm. In addition, she taught Sunday school, took Bible courses, and was 4-H project leader, all while working full-time and helping out at the farm. However, she never held herself in high esteem. She could have this tough as nails exterior while at the same time always desiring approval from her family and peers.

Wanda had a wonderful life growing up with her parents and four siblings. She had two older brothers and two younger sisters. Her oldest brother, Philip, was also adopted. She loved her parents and family dearly. When she was five years old, just before starting school, her parents sat her down and told her she was adopted and that they had chosen her. It made her feel very special. Her parents never treated her any differently than any of their other children.

After they told her she was adopted, it was never brought up again and never mentioned by her parents or the other Keller children except for one time. Wanda never forgot the second time her mother talked to her about being adopted. It had been a particular difficult day for them both as Wanda could be pretty hard headed and stubborn. Her mother knew it was time to have a heart-to-heart talk. She told Wanda, "Remember, Wanda, we didn't HAVE to bring you home. We had a chance to see you first, and we CHOSE you." She then gave Wanda a copy of the book *Peck's Bad Boy* to read about being mischievous. Wanda felt so much better after that but even though it was not discussed, she never forgot.

The adoption, however, was not a secret in the community. At social events, Wanda, as a young child, would sometimes hear people whispering not so quietly, "Now, which one is the adopted girl?" That stuck with her throughout her entire life.

Wanda shared a memorable event about a day at school when a classmate named Jack "just once" made a nasty remark about her adoption. "I was a real tomboy, and I really pounced on him," she said. "The teacher broke up the fight and disciplined me but not Jack. I never did know if the teacher knew the reason for my behavior, but Jack never mentioned my being adopted again."

Wanda never wanted her parents to feel bad that she yearned to find out about her birth parents. But a part of her was missing. She always wanted to know who she was and was especially curious about her birth mother. Growing up on a farm in the depression years wasn't fun, but everyone was in the same boat. She wondered as she carried in the wood and filled the coal oil lamps if her birth mother lived in a mansion on a hill.

When Wanda turned eighteen, her parents gave her the adoption papers. These were the papers my mother copied and gave to each of us kids. The papers revealed that she was born in Kansas City, Missouri, and that her birth name was Marcia Hendrickson. Among the adoption papers was a letter to

Grandma Keller from a woman at the adoption agency and a pathology report showing two blood tests. The lab reports were signed by a Dr. E. L. Stewart and showed the results for two patients. The results were both negative. One was for patient Marcia, and the second was for patient Leona May. This was the only place in all the documents that a name was given for either parent. A third document gave the father's and mother's ages as twenty-one and seventeen respectively, being country reared and of English ancestry. That was it.

In 1946 at the age of twenty, Wanda made a trip with her friend Babe and Babe's parents to California. Wanda and Babe were going to check out the possibility of living and working there. They eventually found work in a lemon packing company but it definitely wasn't the job of their dreams. One day they decided for fun to have their futures read by a fortune teller. Neither of them had ever done anything like that before and sure never heard of anything so crazy back in Kansas. They felt kind of silly but they were adventurous and egged each other on. They opened the door with the neon sign of a glowing hand and words "Fortune Teller." The girls locked arms and entered, pushing and pulling each other through the doorway.

Never one to pass up a dare, Wanda went first and sat across from the fortune teller. The medium asked for her hand, turned it palm side up, and examined it closely. What happened next caught Wanda completely off guard. The medium told Wanda she could see that she had been adopted and longed to find her birth mother. Wanda's mouth was agape. "How could you know that?" she asked in total shock.

Even Babe didn't know Wanda had been adopted. She was as shocked as Wanda at this revelation by the medium. Continuing to read her palm, the fortune teller promised that one day Wanda would find her birth mother. The medium amazed Wanda with many other facts and predictions, of which many were to come true, such as she was going to marry a farm boy back in Kansas that she was already smitten with and would have three children, two girls and a boy. The reading shook Wanda, and she was ready to leave as soon as Babe's fortune was told.

The fortune teller took Babe's hand and Babe gave Wanda a worrisome smile. After the revelation Wanda had been given she wasn't sure what she would be told. The medium told Babe she would marry and find happiness in California and not return to Kansas. Interestingly, Babe found a job she liked and stayed. She got married, and lived the rest of her life as a Californian.

Wanda's brother John Vernon was in the Navy during World War II and she hadn't seen him in a couple years. He wrote Wanda and said he was returning home to port in Oakland, California and asked her to meet him and go home with him. There was a certain young farm boy back home that Wanda liked and missed so she took John Vernon up on his offer.

A couple weeks later, Wanda and her brother headed back to Kansas. The two made the long train ride home, but the final leg didn't go through Topeka. They would have to go to Kansas City to the Union Station and spend the night then catch a bus back to Topeka. John Vernon asked Wanda if she was game to get off at Osage City, Kansas and hitchhike a ride the last 50 miles to Topeka. She said sure never to let her big brother down. Trunks and bags in hand, they deboarded the train. John Vernon in his Navy uniform and Wanda in her high heels, they struggled from the train station to the road side. "Show some leg, girl, like they do in the movies. We want to get home tonight," John Vernon teased his sister and chuckled his ornery laugh.

Wanda blushed and slugged her brother's arm. She must have looked pretty good though because the first car that came along stopped. A nice young man was heading to Topeka and offered to take them. He helped John Vernon pile in the baggage, they climbed in the car, and he gave them a fast ride to Topeka that made her extremely nervous. Fortunately, some cousins were at a dance in Topeka and gave the two a ride home. This was

Wanda's one and only experience hitchhiking and she would never forget it. She warned her children, "You are never to hitchhike!"

Upon her return to Kansas, Wanda started seriously seeing the young man she had dated before leaving for California. Leroy Parr was a handsome young farmer from Rossville, a neighboring town. He was playing summer league baseball when he met Wanda's sister Naomi. The two dated a few times when Leroy's cousin Red asked Leroy if he would talk to Naomi about setting him up on a date with Wanda. Wanda agreed and the two couples went out on a double date.

Wanda and Naomi were always close, being just a year apart in age. They were in the same grade in high school because Naomi was moved up a grade since she was the only student her age in the one-room school house they attended as children. Naomi shared after their double date that she thought Wanda actually was a better fit for Leroy with their common interest in sports, the outdoors, and the farm. Wanda had to admit she was attracted to the blondish-brown haired, blue-eyed, athletic, mischievous farm boy over Red. Naomi told Leroy she thought he should ask Wanda out. So the match was made. Leroy fell for Wanda and even wrote her while she was in California, saying he was waiting for her return. The two fell in love and were married in 1946. The first of the fortune teller's predictions came true.

After returning home, Wanda never talked much about the fortune teller's predictions. The only person Wanda told about the prediction of finding her birth mother was her best friend Genevieve. This was a secret they kept between themselves. Wanda had many long conversations over the years with Genevieve about being adopted and her feelings about being given up by her birth mother. Genevieve understood how hard this was for Wanda and was a true friend to listen, comfort, and just be there for her, as was Wanda for her when she needed her.

Throughout my mother's adult life, she tried to glean information about her birth parents but had not had any luck. On vacations she would look in the phone book in the motel room and scan for the last name Hendrickson. One family vacation we went to California to go to Disneyland. We drove the entire way in our green 1965 Chevy Impala with us kids squabbling most of the way. We stayed in a hotel in Albuquerque, New Mexico, and were excited they had an indoor swimming pool. Dad took us to go swimming but the pool was filled with a slimy, green moss. So much for swimming.

When we got back to the room, my mother was looking through the phone book and searching for the last name Hendrickson. She closed the book and said, "I was looking to see if there are any Hendricksons living here. No such luck. You never know, I thought maybe my birth mother might have moved to New Mexico from Missouri."

Amazing that even on a family outing with all that was going on, she still had her birth mother and being adopted on her mind. It just showed how strong her desire was to find anything out about her birth parents. Surprisingly, the spelling of Hendrickson is not that common and she never was able to find anyone to call to ask if they had a family member named Leona.

Any TV show or magazine article about adopted children finding their birth parents caught my mother's eye. There was a show called "Reunion" that my mother never missed. It was about people who were looking for their children given up for adoption or their birth parents. They could give a little about themselves, who they were looking for, and leave contact information. Mother always had her pencil and paper out in case someone was looking for her. She once read in *Reader's Digest* how one man tracked down his birth father. He started an organization to help others find their parents. Even though it was kind of expensive, Mother joined the organization for suggestions. They told her to check to see if she could get more information about her birth mother through Missouri state records, but Missouri adoption records were sealed and not available. It was a dead end, and she was quite frustrated.

Now here at the Kansas Historical Society, I am thinking to myself, "Could it be possible all this time her birth mother was actually from Kansas and not Missouri?"

Chapter 6

My tour guide showed me how to access the information for the census. By federal law, the census is closed for 72 years. This meant the only past censuses available in 1990 were the censuses every five years from 1865 through 1915. I thought, "That could work!" Knowing from the adoption papers that my grandmother was seventeen years old when she had my mother in 1925, she would have been two or three years old in 1910.

We found the 1910 Kansas census and I asked my new friend how to search for a particular last name that starts with the letter "H." "Well, I have good news and bad news," she said. "The good news is the census is alphabetical by first letter of the last name. The bad news is all the names starting with the letter 'H' are not alphabetical. All the names starting with 'H' are lumped together so the first entry might be Humphrey and next entry will be Harvey. You will just have to scroll through each name to look for the one you are searching."

As if this wasn't bad enough she added, "Oh, and they are all listed by county so you will have to search the 'H's' county by county."

"Oh wow, that could take days," I said to her.

She chuckled and said, "That is why we have such comfortable chairs," as she pointed to the hard, wooden, straight-back chairs with no cushions stationed in front of the microfiche viewers.

This was the end of the tour. I thanked her for her time and all her helpful information that would be so beneficial for my lesson plans. I told her I was going to stay and check out the census. She wished me good luck and I started my task at hand. Methodically, I started going through the "H's" county by county, Allen, Anderson, Atchison.... The name I was looking for was not to be found. I spent the next four hours reading the names Hubbard, Hilliard, Hanks, Hoover, Herbert, on and on but no Hendricksons. It was so frustrating that they weren't in alphabetical order.

It was painstaking and nothing even came close. There are 105 counties in Kansas. I was up to Kiowa County, about halfway through, as the day was coming to an end. The state historical society building was closing for the day, and I decided to shut down shop and try again another day.

Chapter 7

The next morning I found myself again sitting in front of the microfiche viewer in that most uncomfortable chair. As I was getting ready to leave my condo that morning, I thought about what a crazy way this was to spend the last days of my spring break. At the same time, I felt I had started a mission and needed to see it through. I had become pretty adept at the microfiche and quickly loaded the next county, Labette, in the viewer. Off we went, Herbers, Hanks, Hoobler, Hess.... I had found a couple Hendrix, Hendricks, Henderson but still no Hendrickson.

I had been at it for about an hour and had reached Montgomery County. I was methodically trucking along when a name jumped out at me. It was Hendrickson. I looked at it again and sure enough, there was the name HENDRICKSON! I would have let out a yelp if I hadn't been in that mammoth cave of a room and hadn't thought I would get my hand slapped for talking or at least a mean glare from the other four or five patrons in the room. My heart was pounding as I looked closer at the information.

There were two listings for that last name Hendrickson. One was a James Hendrickson and the other was Hugh Hendrickson. I looked at both closely. There was no Leona listed in James' family members. In the other entry, Hugh was listed as the father, 43 years of age and his wife, Anna, was 28 years old. They had three children: Iva, 10 years old; Louis, 6 years old; and Ona, 2 years old. No Leona. I was disappointed and then it hit me smack upside the head. Could Ona be short for Leona? The age was right.

My tour guide had shown me the forms available to write down information for each census. She gave me one with the heading *1910 United States Census*. There were blanks to write the microfilm roll number, state, county, and town or township. Then there were columns with headings to write all kinds of information found on the census, such as name, age, occupation, education, farm/home, and more.

I quickly took out a pencil and the paper the tour guide gave me the day before from my backpack and began jotting down all the information listed for the Hugh Hendrickson family from Montgomery County. They were from the small town of Havana, Kansas. The census gave information about their farm. They had 80 acres of land with 10 acres in corn, 15 acres in forage and grains, and 55 acres of native pasture. They had three horses, two cows, and one pig. I wrote down all the family members' names and ages, making sure I had every bit of information.

Now that I had a name and town, I decided to take this information and keep digging. What if I were to check the 1915 census for Montgomery County and see if the Hendrickson family was listed? Being familiar with the microfiche, I quickly swapped out the 1910 census for the 1915 census. Knowing to look for Montgomery County, I quickly scrolled down to that section of the census.

I found the "H's" and started the search for Hendrickson. It didn't take me too long and there was the name Hendrickson listed. It was James Hendrickson again. Hugh was not entered right after James as it had been before. "Oh no, could they have moved?" I continued searching, hoping Hugh was just listed later in the census.

About fifteen entries later I found another Hendrickson listed. It was C. H. Hendrickson. Could the H be for Hugh?

YES! His wife's name was Anna. They now were 48 and 33 years of age so it had to be them. Okay, what about their children? This time there were four listed: Iva U., 13; Louis, 10; Leona, 7; and Grace, 3. There it was, LEONA! Ona was Leona!

Once again my heart pounded as I read on about the Hendrickson family. The family seemed to be doing pretty well as they had increased their farm by 45 acres to a total of 125 acres. This census was much more detailed. They had 50 bushels of corn on hand, three tons of prairie hay, 250 lb. of butter, 25 chickens, three horses, one mule, two milk cows, three other cows, 21 pigs, and two dogs. Who would ever thought on a census they would list number of dogs. I was ecstatic finding Leona's name and this new information and decided to run with it. I didn't care to spend any more time in that hard, wooden chair. If nothing panned out with this lead, at least knew where I left off.

Chapter 8

Montgomery County, Kansas, wasn't all that unfamiliar to me. It was in southeast Kansas and shared a border with Oklahoma. Before I got my teaching certification, I worked for four years as the county extension agricultural and 4-H agent in Elk County, Kansas, and lived in the town of Howard.

It also just so happened that Montgomery butted up against Elk County on Elk's southeast corner. I had traveled through Montgomery County a lot but I had never heard of the town of Havana. As soon as I got home, I pulled out my Rand McNally Road Atlas and looked for the Kansas map. I knew that Independence, Kansas, was the Montgomery County seat. Many times I had driven the county extension pickup over to meetings in Independence with other extension agents.

Looking in the index, sure enough there was a Havana, Kansas, population 191. I got the coordinates and found Havana on the map. It was in the southwest corner of the county and only about 15 miles from the Oklahoma border. Havana actually was right on the border between Montgomery County and Chautauqua County. Chautauqua was the county directly south of Elk County. Havana was only ten miles to the west of Sedan, Kansas, the county seat of Chautauqua County. "Really?" I thought. "This is crazy!"

I thought back to my four years working in Howard. It was definitely an interesting time in my life, and southeast Kansas was quite different than where I was raised. I was 26 years old when I got the job and moved there. The county population was about 800 and Elk County had the distinction of being the oldest average-age population of any county in the state. It was about 60 miles to Wichita or any other large city.

Being such a small community and a very old population, the youngsters couldn't wait to "get out of Dodge," and there weren't many single people in their mid-20s. The Elk County kids either got married right out of high school (if not before) or headed to the bright lights where there were better jobs and a heck of a lot more to do.

Interestingly enough though, I made some of my lifelong friends while working there. Rachelle Mengarelli, Elk County Extension Home Economist and Director, was just a year younger than me and single. We became best friends. She had been there a few years already and had developed a circle of about ten single friends from a 30-mile radius of Howard who got together almost every weekend. I was welcomed into the group.

Three of these friends were Brent, Ed, and Sherry who all had lived in Sedan. So many Saturday nights were spent in Sedan, playing cards and games or watching Kansas State University football or basketball games on TV. (Most of us had all graduated from KSU and to this day still have season tickets together.) I even went to the Sedan Baptist church one Sunday morning with Sherry. Could my grandmother really have been born just ten miles from Sedan, Kansas, a place so familiar to me?

I ran out of time to find the answer to this question. With spring break rapidly coming to a close, I really didn't have time to keep researching and trying to get more answers. I needed to get ready for the last quarter of school and focus on my lesson plans. Once school was out, I would have more time for my search. I had waited this long, I could wait a little longer.

Chapter 9

As school started back up after spring break, things got very hectic. I almost forgot about my search for Leona but of course it never totally left my mind. Every time I went into my office I would see the folder with the information I had gleaned over spring break just sitting there waiting for me.

The final quarter of school went very quickly. After finishing up my first full year of teaching, I realized what a wonderful year I had and would miss my "kids." I couldn't have asked for a better group of third grade students in my first class. My lessons on the history of Topeka went great too.

Now that school was out, it was almost as if that folder on my desk were calling me. It was the first Saturday morning of summer vacation. What to do next now that I knew a Leona Hendrickson had lived in Havana, Kansas? None of my friends still lived in the area as we had all moved and scattered to other parts of the state. We couldn't wait to "get out of Dodge" either. So I couldn't ask one of them to check it out for me. I had to think of another strategy.

After giving it some thought, an idea popped into my head. Having grown up in a small Kansas town myself, I knew that if they had a local post office in Havana, the postmaster would be the best person to know any Hendricksons in the town. The post office should be open for a little while on Saturday morning if it was like back home. I called information and sure enough, Havana still had a post office. Guess it wasn't a ghost town yet. I dialed the number. The phone rang and a very nice lady answered, "Hello, this is the Havana Post Office. How may I help you?"

I had actually thought through what I was going to say. "Yes, thank you. I do hope you can help me. I am doing some research about my family history. I live in Topeka, Kansas, but I believe I might have some family from Havana. Do you know if there are any Hendricksons that live in Havana?"

"No, I don't recognize that name," the sweet-voiced Kansas postmistress said.

She sounded just like the postmistress back in my hometown where I grew up. I could almost hear Pauline's voice answering the phone. This lady was just as kind as Pauline with a smile in her voice. She was apologetic that she didn't know anyone by that name. She stopped and said, "I haven't lived here all my life and don't recognize that name. But I do know someone who might be able to help. You need to call and talk to Dennis Wade. We all call him Bus. He grew up here and knows everybody in town and most of the ones in the cemetery, too."

She cackled and went on to tell me that he was retired but still takes care of the cemetery. She said, "Everybody in the area knows Bus. He's a good ol' guy and if there was a Hendrickson that lived in these parts, he would be able to tell you. Let me give you his phone number."

Amazingly she gave me his phone number and said she knew he would be glad to help me if he could. I thanked her for being so kind and for her help. I hadn't gotten any information about the Hendrickson name but figured I might as well call good ol' Bus.

The telephone rang twice and a very pleasant older lady's voice came across the line.

"Hello?"

"Hi, could I speak to Bus Wade, please?" I asked.

She said, "Oh, I am so sorry. Bus isn't here right now. Could I give him a message?"

"Well, you might be able to help me."

I gave her my name and continued, "I have been doing some research about my family history. I think maybe some of my family might have been from Havana. I called the post office and the nice lady there told me Bus Wade would be the person to ask and she gave me your number. I hope you don't mind my calling."

"Why not at all, young man. Anything we can do to help you find your family would be just fine by me."

"Well, the last name of some of my relatives on my mother's side of the family that I have traced is Hendrickson. I believe there might have been some Hendricksons that lived in your area. You wouldn't happen to know if there is anyone with that last name that lives or used to live in Havana?" I asked.

"Oh honey, I sure don't, but Emily was right, my husband Bus sure would," she chuckled. "That man knows everybody. He has lived here his whole life and takes care of the cemetery so he knows everyone that ever lived and died here."

"Do you have any idea when Bus might be home and I could reach him?"

"How about you give me your number and I will have Bus call you when he gets back in."

"Oh, thank you so much. I do live in Topeka and it is long distance. Why don't I call back? When would be a good time to call?"

"Okay, honey. He will be back this evening. Could you call between say 6:00 and 7:00?"

"Yes, that will be great. I really appreciate it. Goodbye."

I thought, "Looks like I am going to have to wait a little bit longer to see if he knows a Leona Hendrickson."

It seemed like time passed by slowly waiting for 6:00 to arrive. I waited until about 6:15 not to seem too anxious. I dialed the number again and the phone rang.

"Hello?"

"Hi, is this Mr. Wade?"

A man with a wonderful twang in his voice says, "Yep, sure is. Did you call earlier? My wife told me someone had called and was lookin' for some kinfolk here in Havana. Maybe I can he'p you."

"Yes, that's me, Mr. Wade. Thanks so much. I am researching my family history, and I think there might have been some relatives on my mother's side of the family that lived in Havana named Hendrickson. Do you know if there ever were any Hendricksons from Havana?"

"Well, first of all just call me Bus. Yep, there's an old Hendrickson farmstead and also a house here in town that everyone from way back called the Hendrickson place. There were a bunch of them Hendricksons around here at one time when I was a young'un. But nobody with the last name Hendrickson still lives around here anymore."

"Do you know if there was ever a Hugh and Anna Hendrickson that lived there?" I asked.

He stopped to think and he said, "Well, there was brothers James and Clark Hendrickson. Clark was married to an Anna. They are all buried in the Havana Cemetery and died a long time ago."

"Okay," I thought to myself, "that makes sense. The 1910 census said Hugh and Anna Hendrickson but the 1915 census had C. H. and Anna Hendrickson. C. H. must stand for Clark Hugh."

Bus went on, "I don't know nothing about Clark's kinfolk but I do know one of James' sons. Last I knew, he lived in Wichita. His name is Claude. He's a little older than me but we grew up together. I could look up his phone number if you want. I know I have it around here some place. I try to keep up on information that I can about relatives of people buried in the cemetery."

That familiar feeling of my heart pounding began as I was feeling like I had struck gold.

Bus asked if I could hold while he looked up the number. I wish I could have had a video of my face throughout this whole conversation. How was this happening so easily? Next thing I knew, Bus was back on the phone reading to me the phone number for Claude Hendrickson in Wichita. I thanked him profusely and he said he hoped it helped.

With another phone number in front of me, I wasn't about to stop now. Ring, ring, ring.

Chapter 10

"Hello?"

"Hi, is this Claude Hendrickson?"

"Yes, it is. How can I help you?" the elderly man's voice on the other end of the phone asked.

I didn't feel comfortable saying right up front that I was looking for Leona and why so I said, "My name is KelLee Parr, and I am doing some genealogical research on my family tree and I have come across the name Hendrickson as a possible branch."

"Well, I don't know too much about the family history so probably can't help you much." He sounded very cautious and leery of this stranger calling and asking about his family.

"I don't know if you know Bus Wade from Havana but he gave me your phone number. I called and talked to him because I had traced back some family history matching the last name Hendrickson to Havana. He told me that your father James and Uncle Clark had lived in Havana. Bus said he grew up with you."

Warming up Claude said, "Oh yes, I remember Bus. He is a good ol' boy. I did grow up in Havana."

"That's great. Would you mind my taking a little of your time and asking a few questions?" I asked.

"No, that's fine. What would you like to know?"

"Well, could you start by telling me about your grandparents and your family?"

"Sure, my grandfather was Amariah Hendrickson, and my grandmother, Mary Ann. My father was born in Havana. He grew up there, and I was born and raised there on a farm. But I moved to Wichita when I got out of the service."

"That is great. I think we might be distant cousins. Through my research I found some connection to the last name Hendrickson on my mother's side and through the census at the Kansas Historical Society found there were Hendricksons that were from Havana. I called the post office in Havana and the nice lady there hooked me up with Bus."

Claude became much more comfortable and proceeded to tell me all about his dad. I didn't want to interrupt him as I took down some notes about his family. I was having a hard time focusing on what he was telling me when all I wanted to do was ask about his Uncle Clark and if he had a cousin named Leona, but I was polite and listened. He went on to tell me all about his family and kids and all his brother and sisters' kids and where they were located. He said he had a sister in Arizona that was working on a Hendrickson family tree."

"Oh that's interesting. Maybe I could talk to her sometime," I said.

"Yes, I am sure she would love to talk to you about the family. She can tell you a lot more about my grandparents. I do know they moved their family to Havana from Illinois in the 1870s to farm."

So I asked if they had other children besides his dad and his Uncle Clark.

"Yes, my grandparents had eight children. Hugh was born in Illinois and died as a small child. Aunt Alice, Uncle Clark, Aunt Margaret Elizabeth, and Uncle Milton were also born in Illinois. Aunt Anna, my dad James, and Uncle George Hamilton were all born in Kansas. My dad and Uncle Clark stayed and farmed around Havana. Most of the cousins are now scattered all over the country."

"How interesting. So your dad and your Uncle Clark were farmers?" I shared, "My dad is a farmer, and I grew up on a farm in northeast Kansas."

I used this as my chance to get to the question I really wanted to ask. "Could you tell me more about your Uncle Clark and his family?"

He said, "Well, I don't remember Uncle Clark. He was named Clark Hugh after his older brother that died. Uncle Clark died when I was pretty little. Think he had the fever or something."

"His wife's name was Anna," he continued. "I remember Dad said things were pretty tough for Aunt Anna and her kids after Uncle Clark died. He tried to help them as much as he could. We cousins used to be pretty close and got together most weekends at our grams and gramps growing up. We do try to stay in touch some still but don't get together much anymore. Haven't seen any of Uncle Clark's kids for a long time."

Do I dare ask? "So Mr. Hendrickson, you said your Uncle Clark and Aunt Anna had five children?"

"Yes, he had five kids. Iva, Louis, Leona, Goldie, and Dale. We always called Dale, 'Bud.'"

My heart stopped. There it was: "Leona." The first time I actually had heard the name Leona out loud. "Are any of these cousins still alive?"

"Well, Goldie died when she was in her late twenties I think it was. Iva and Louis have passed on as well. Iva lived in Garnett, Kansas, and Louis lived in Oregon. All the rest of the family moved out to be close to Louis and are all still out there."

I know I was about to hyperventilate, but I asked calmly, "So Leona and Bud live in Oregon?"

"No, Bud lives in Klamath Falls, Oregon, but Leona actually lives in California in a little town called Dorris, just south of the Oregon/California border. Her last name is Britches. Don't know when was the last time we got together but we write and stay in touch some."

Leona's alive! My mind raced as I was taking notes shakily and he gave me another possible piece to the puzzle.

"That's so interesting," I said. "I love hearing all about your family. I so appreciate all you've shared about your family and it's so fascinating. I can't wait to do more research and see if we are related. This is so helpful. Do you think your sister in Arizona might be able to give me more information?"

"Oh yes, I'm sure she would love to talk to you about our family."

"That would be wonderful," I said. "What about your cousins Leona or Bud? Do you think they might be able to give me more information about their side of the Hendrickson family?"

"Well, they are pretty private people. I haven't talked to them in a while and I need to give them a call. How about you give me your information to give them and they can contact you if they want?"

That wasn't what I really wanted but it was fair. I didn't want to be too pushy. "Sure, that sounds great."

He said, "Let me grab a pencil and paper."

There was a long pause and I could hear footsteps as I imagined Claude walking over to his old, roll-top desk and retrieving pencil and paper. I heard the footsteps getting closer and then the phone receiver being picked up off the table. "Okay, I'm ready."

I gave Claude my mailing address and phone number. Though I was having a hard time containing my enthusiasm, I calmly told him again that I really had enjoyed learning about his family history. "Thank you so much for your time. Would you mind if I contact you again if I come across any more information or have more questions?"

He politely said, "You are quite welcome, young man. Please don't hesitate to call anytime if you have more questions. Hope this has been helpful in your research. Have a good evening."

I thought to myself, "I hope so too."

I signed off, "Thanks again and have a good evening." Click.

Chapter 11

After talking to Claude, I picked up my Rand McNally and turned to California. Where the heck was Dorris, California? It was a small town with a population of 899 in northeastern California on the Oregon border. Just as Claude said, the largest city nearby was Klamath Falls, Oregon, about 20 miles to the northeast. I called information for Dorris and asked for the phone number of a Leona Britches. There was no listing.

Of course, I still had no idea if this was actually the person I was looking for. Should I try to get in touch with Leona? I turned to my friend Ellen who was out on her patio planting flowers and enjoying her Saturday evening. She beamed with anticipation when I asked her if she would like to know about my latest discoveries on my search. I shared with her about my conversations with my new friends Bus and Claude.

Ellen was dumbfounded. She could hardly believe what I had uncovered in such a short time. She was as excited as I was and her genuine enthusiasm was quite reaffirming. It was really nice to have someone to share all that was happening and get another person's opinion on what I should do next. I trusted her insight.

"What should I do?" I asked Ellen. "I know Leona's last name is Britches. I tried calling information and there was nobody listed. I could call and ask information for a Dale Hendrickson. Claude said Bud lived in Klamath Falls. Do I try and contact Leona through Bud?"

Ellen pondered the question for a little while. She was a fount of wisdom and I appreciated her thoughtful responses because every idea ran through the filter of her own adoption and she could foresee issues I couldn't. She explained there could be ramifications if I contacted Leona or Bud. She shared her feelings of wanting to know her birth mother but cautioned how difficult it might be to be rejected. "We don't even know if this is your grandmother," she said. "And you say Claude said he would give Leona or Bud your information?"

"Yes, that's what he said but how do I know he really will or if Leona or Bud would even contact me?"

"Well you don't, but I think you might want to give them a chance first. I know you are anxious to keep going with this but it might be best to go slow," she advised.

She was right. I needed to take a little time and think this through and give Leona and Bud a chance to contact me. It seemed too awkward to contact Bud, even if I could find him, and ask about Leona. "Did your sister have a baby in 1925?" No, I didn't think that would be good.

As difficult as it was, I had to be patient and see what would happen next. It was time to enjoy the rest of my summer.

Chapter 12

After school was out, I spent an extra week at school getting my room in order. Also to earn a little extra money, I served on the social studies standards writing committee for our district's third grade curriculum. This consumed two weeks through the first week of June so my "real" vacation started the following week.

My time to relax was during the summer, but I liked to get all the planning done for the next year early so I didn't have it hanging over my head. This first summer break I found the best time to get things done was right after school was out when I was still in "work" mode rather than "vacation" mode. It was always amazing to me how much I could accomplish in those first few weeks after school was out while my body and mind were still in "work" mode.

I always thought teaching would be so great because of the summer breaks, not realizing how exhausting it was to teach and be in charge of 25 students eight hours a day, planning lessons, teaching so many subjects, and managing students' behavior for nine long months. I quickly understood how important it was to get rejuvenated for the next group in the fall. This break was the only thing standing between me and burnout.

On a Friday I wrapped up my committee work and headed home, rejoicing that I didn't have to think about school work for a few weeks. I climbed the stairs to my condo and unlocked my door. I peered at Ellen's patio and she wasn't home yet. So I went in my condo, shut the door, and carried my school bag into my office.

I tossed my bag into the corner, knowing I was officially off duty for a few weeks. The notes on my desk from my conversations with Bus and Claude caught my attention. I was flooded with excitement as I recalled how much progress I'd made toward finding my mother's birth mother. I had not heard from Leona or Bud since I spoke to Claude. Maybe I should call Claude back? My weekend was busy but now I was going to have time to continue my search. However, I still planned to keep the research to myself until I knew more.

The next Monday I drove to my parents' farm. It was about an hour's drive from Topeka. Over the next few weeks, I would be going out to the farm to help my dad. We had to check the cattle in the pastures and start cutting and baling the alfalfa and brome hay for their feed in the winter.

Thankfully we no longer baled the small square bales like when I was a kid. It was exhausting hauling them into the barn. Of course as soon as I went off to college, Dad decided it was time to buy "one of those balers that makes big round hay bales." With it he could make gigantic round bales of hay to haul with the tractor and feed the cattle by himself. What a huge time and labor saver not having to lift the small square bales by hand.

There was always plenty to do out at the farm and this day was no different. The huge garden my folks always planted needed weeding, and the radishes and lettuce needed to be harvested. And the huge five acres of yard needed to be mowed—mowing was my least favorite chore. Mother put out a big spread for lunch: smothered home-grown steak with mashed potatoes and gravy. She made my favorite raspberry jello salad with ice cream, bananas, and pineapple.

As we sat down to the table, my mother had the TV on to watch "Days of Our Lives" because she couldn't miss one moment of John's, Marlena's, Bo's and Hope's turbulent lives. During commercials, I told my parents about my plans to go to Florida at the end of the month to visit Jane. I couldn't wait to see her and get to the beach. The lunch was yummy as always and was topped off with homemade cherry pie just out of the oven. We talked about everything except my clandestine research project trying to locate my mother's birth mother.

After a long day of sweating from working outside, I had accomplished a great deal and was ready to head home. Mother wanted me to stay for supper but I really wanted to get home to meet up with some friends that night. So I took my Tupperware dish with goodies, including another piece of cherry pie, and some of the fresh produce from the garden and headed back home over the gravel roads with dust flying.

I always enjoyed the 30-mile trip to and from the farm. I got to travel through my old hometown of Rossville where I went to high school. It was always fun to be back and see familiar surroundings and wave at friends. Because it was such a small town, I was related to most of them.

The last ten miles of the trip to our farm were gravel roads. I remember as a kid all the Sunday trips we made to spend time with Grandma and Grandpa Keller on the farm with all the uncles, aunts, and cousins. It seemed like the drive took forever back then. Now I loved the peace and quiet and beauty of the countryside. Mostly it was rolling hills with pastures dotted with grazing cattle.

Arriving home that evening, I parked my pickup in my designated carport and headed with my haul of goodies from the farm to the breezeway between the condos where all the mailboxes were lined up on the north wall. I unlocked my mailbox and grabbed my mail. I walked across the green carpet that looked like artificial grass. The "grass" continued to grow on each stair step leading up to my second floor condo. My hands were full but as I was climbing the green stairs, I could see on top of the pile of mail one small white envelope. It was addressed to Kelly Parr. The return address in all capped letters read: LEONA BRETCHES, P.O. BOX 555, DORRIS, CA 96023.

Chapter 13

What the heck! It was a letter from Leona! I got a letter from Leona! Leona's last name was Bretches, not Britches! Claude had spelled it wrong. I ran up the rest of the flight of stairs to my apartment, threw open the door, dropped all my goodies on the table and ran to the desk to get my letter opener. I carefully sliced the top of the envelope open and pulled out the letter.

It read:

June 4, 1991

Mr. Parr:

I got word you was wanting to get in touch with me, something about the Family Hendrickson tree. My cousin in Ariz. Was working on one. My father Clark Hue Hendrickson married my mother Anna Richards in 1898. They had 5 children, Iva, Louis, Leona, Goldie, and Dale. Dale and I are only ones still living. And we are not interested in family tree. If you want to get in touch with me my address is:

Leona Bretches

P.O. Box 555

Dorris, CA 96023

There it is! The answer I have been waiting for and my doorway to contact Leona to ask if she is my grandmother. I was shaking and must have read the letter three or four times. I wanted to tell someone. I ran next door and Ellen wasn't home yet. Should I call one of my sisters? No. I decided to wait because this might not be THE Leona I was looking for and why get her hopes up.

I picked up the leftovers from the farm and put the dishes in the fridge. I set the radishes and fresh green beans Mother had given me from the garden into the sink. I ran to my office and grabbed pen and paper to start a letter to Leona. This was going to need to be worded quite delicately. How do you broach the subject to someone? "Hey by the way, did you have a kid 66 years ago that you put up for adoption?" I had no way of knowing if she was the right person and also what if she was the wrong person? She might be very offended.

Thinking about writing Leona made me extremely nervous. I had dreamed of this moment for some time but not really thought about what I would actually say in a letter.

After several drafts, I wrote:

Dear Mrs. Bretches,

My name is KelLee Parr. Thank you for writing to me. I have been doing some research trying to locate my birth grandmother. My mother was adopted and has always wanted to learn more about her mother. In doing research using the adoption papers my grandparents gave to my mother, I was able to figure out the name of my mother's birth mother. Her name was Leona May Hendrickson. We know my mother was born in Kansas City, Missouri, but Missouri records are sealed so we had no way of knowing where Leona lived. I happened to think possibly she was from Kansas rather than Missouri so I started researching at the Kansas State Historical Society. I happened across a Hendrickson family from Havana, Kansas, in the 1910 and 1915 censuses. They had a daughter listed as Ona in 1910 and Leona in 1915. This would be about the right age to be my grandmother.

I was able to speak to a Mr. Bus Wade from Havana and asked if he had heard of the Hendrickson family. He was able to get me in touch with a Claude Hendrickson in Wichita, Kansas. I spoke to your cousin Claude, telling him I was doing research on my family tree but did not tell him specifically why, just that I thought I might have some relationship to the Hendrickson family. He told me all about your grandparents and his family. He then was able to tell me about your parents Clark and Anna Hendrickson and their children. He told me about your siblings and that you and Dale (he said he is called Bud) lived in California. Again, I never told Claude that I was searching for a Leona May Hendrickson specifically or why because I wanted to protect her privacy.

Like I mentioned, I don't know if you are the Leona I am looking for who had a daughter born February 14, 1925. If this is not you, I apologize for the trouble. If by chance you are my grandmother, I understand if you are not interested in contacting me back. I do hope you would though.

Just so you know in case you are the Leona I am looking for and would like to know, my mother was raised on a farm by a loving couple from northeast Kansas. My grandparents were wonderful people and loved all their children very much and equally. They had two adopted children and three of their own naturally. My mother has two older brothers and two younger sisters. My mother married in 1946 and has three children, my two older sisters and me. She also has two grandchildren. My dad is a farmer and my parents live on the farm where my mother grew up.

I wanted to tell you this information in case you are the Leona I am looking for just so you know a little about my mother's background and to know she has had a wonderful life and family. She would really love to find her birth mother, get to know her, and complete her family. It has been her lifelong desire to know her birth mother.

Again, thank you for your time and I hope to hear from you.

Sincerely,

KelLee Parr

Topeka, Kansas

After I finished what felt like countless drafts, Ellen's door was open so she was home. I dashed next door and she was sitting out on the deck with cigarette in hand, reading a book. I asked if she would mind reading something. I showed her the letter that had arrived that day. Her mouth literally dropped open as she read it and looked up at me. "Do you think this is her?

"I don't know, but I have to find out," I said. "I am thinking it has to be. I wrote her a letter back and would you mind reading what I wrote? See if you think it sounds okay and appropriate."

I handed her my letter and Ellen took one last drag on her cigarette. She stamped it out in the ashtray and blew the smoke out of the side of her mouth away from me as she always did to avoid smoke in my face. She sat back and read the letter with no expression. I was thinking maybe I needed to dial the letter back a little. I didn't want to be rude to someone that was not the Leona I was looking for, or worse yet, scare her off if she WAS my grandmother. It felt like it took an eternity for her to read it. Still no expression. The entire time she read the letter she continued reading with no expression on her face. I was dying. Was it that bad?

When Ellen looked up, there was a little tear in the corner of her eye. "That is beautiful," she said. "I so hope it is her. How could she not write you back? It is perfect, send it just like that."

Later that evening I put the letter in an envelope, addressed it with Leona's name and sealed it. The next day I mailed it. Later that week I headed to Florida to spend a couple weeks with Jane. The long wait began.

Chapter 14

While telling my sister the background of my spring break adventure, the letter from Leona, and my letter back to Leona asking about the secret, the look on Jane's face as the story unraveled was priceless. She was in shock. She had a thousand questions for me, most of which I had no answers. I shared that Ellen was the only person I had told about searching for Leona. "Now you and Ellen both know so you get to share the anxiety of the secret and the wait," I laughed. "And besides, this might be all for naught."

We still had a couple days left before I had to go home. It was great hitting the beach and enjoying the ocean surf, something I sure didn't have in land-locked Kansas. We would usually go out for dinner and Jane would ask me to tell her again about my search for Leona and any details I might have forgotten to share. The anxiety had multiplied with Jane joining me in wondering if a letter from Leona was going to be in my mailbox when I got home or if I would ever hear from Leona.

After a great time visiting my sister, it was time to head home. Jane hugged me at the airport and said, "Now you call me as soon as you get home so I know you are safe and let me know if you hear anything back from your letter!"

Upon landing in Kansas City from Jacksonville on a hot summer day, I had to make the hour and a half drive from the airport to Topeka. My thoughts were racing, wondering if I had received a letter. I knew by the time I got to my condo, Ellen should be home from work. Arriving home I pulled into my carport, grabbed my suitcases, and entered the breezeway where all the condos' silver mailboxes were. I was sure Ellen would have already gotten my mail but I checked the box anyway. It was empty, of course. I climbed the stairs to the second floor open hallway that separated Ellen's and my doors. Dropping my bags in the hallway, I noticed Ellen's wooden door was wide open to let air flow through her condo from her patio through the screen door. Even on a hot summer day, Ellen preferred a fresh breeze over the air conditioning.

I knocked on her door. Ellen was in the kitchen fixing a salad for dinner. When she came to the door with a carrot in one hand and paring knife in the other, she saw it was me and screamed, "You're here!" She quickly unlocked the screen door and turned to run back to the kitchen. You would have thought she had just spotted Bugs Bunny who was after her precious carrot. She yelled, "Come in, come in." As I opened the door and walked in, Ellen hurriedly set the carrot and knife on the counter and disappeared into the back room of her condo.

My anxiety mounted, wondering what was going on with Ellen. She was screaming at the top of her lungs so loudly I am sure the rest of the condo association was ready to call 911. I couldn't understand a word she was saying. She ran from the back room with a stack of mail. "It came! I think the letter you have been waiting for came!"

We both stopped and looked at each other. My heart skipped a beat as she handed me the pile of letters and on top was one small white envelope with my name and address handwritten on it. The return address was from Leona Bretches. Ellen asked if I wanted to sit down to open it. There was no way she was going to let me take the letter without knowing what it said. I looked at her with what I am sure was a look of curiosity, thrill, and anxiety all in one expression, if that is at all possible. It was all based on one little envelope that was postmarked June 29, 1991, Dorris, California.

As I sat down in her living room, I saw my reflection in the mirrored wall Ellen had installed as one of her remodeling projects. There was a slight smile on my face but also a little look of fear. I thought to myself, "Is this what I have been hoping for?" With the letter in hand, I wondered if this was going to be the answer to all my mother's questions or just a dead end.

I could see Ellen was anxious for me to open the letter. "Well, are you going to open it or what?" she finally said, breaking the ice.

I laughed and said, "Guess it is now or never."

Ellen wiped the blade of the knife she had been using to cut the carrots and handed it to me to use as a letter opener. She sat down opposite me and both of us had our eyes glued to the letter as I carefully slit the top of the envelope open and pulled out the letter. One more look at Ellen. We shared nervous smiles without saying anything. I unfolded the letter. The handwritten letter was in ink and looked a little shaky. I read the letter aloud.

June 29, 1991

Mr. KelLee Parr

I am writing this in regards to the letter I received from you. Have tried to call you but no answer. So I will write a few lines.

Yes, I think I am the Leona May you are looking for. Sorry haven't written sooner. This was one subject that was never talked about but never forgotten.

Yes, I would like to meet your mother or at least get a picture and will send you mine.

I am 83 years old and have fairly good health. I have a garden and do my yard work and like to fish and hunt. So you see I am not an indoor person.

If you would like to call me on phone, my number is 555-396-4153. Call so you can get me early of a morning or around 9 p.m.

Hope this finds your mother o.k. I would love to meet you all. My husband passed away 14 years ago this December 14. So x-mas time is a bad time for me. I get along o.k.

Sincerely,

Leona May

Leona Bretches

P.O. Box 555

Dorris, CA 96023

P.S. Dorris is just 20 miles south of Klamath Falls, OR on Highway 97. Population close to 1000, so it is a small town.

I looked up at Ellen. A tear ran down her cheek. "You did it!" she shouted and jumped up and gave me a hug. The feeling of total amazement and joy spread through my whole body. I couldn't believe I had just read a letter from my grandmother. It was hard to wrap my mind around it. Could this be for real? I read the letter again and thanked Ellen for all her help.

Ellen said, "I can't believe you found her. This is so incredible. Now what are you going to do?"

"I had better go call my sister and tell her the news," I said.

My first thoughts were of my mother and how in the world was I going to break this news to her. She was going to be so shocked but so happy. I gave Ellen another hug and opened the screen door to the hallway between our condos. I gathered my luggage marooned in the hall and unlocked the door to my condo. Walking in the door, I dropped my bags on the floor but carefully placed the mail with "the letter" on the kitchen table. I went straight to the phone.

Chapter 15

"Hi, Jane. I made it home safe and sound."

"Oh, thank you so much for calling. I have been wondering if you made it home okay. And I can't stand it. I have been dying to know if you got a letter from Leona," she said excitedly.

Calmly I replied with a dejected tone in my voice, "Well, I checked my mailbox as soon as I got home and it was empty."

I heard a little sigh and "Oh drat" from Jane as I hesitated.

Then I said slowly, building up with excitement, "Yeah, it was a good flight home. It was pretty hot getting to my car. The whole trip I kept thinking how I hoped there would be an answer when I got here. So I came up the stairs after checking my empty mailbox and stopped to talk to Ellen. Oh, I forgot to tell you that she was collecting my mail for me. AND THERE WAS A LETTER FROM LEONA! It is her! Leona May Hendrickson! She is Mother's birth mother! She is our grandmother! Can you believe it?"

Jane screamed in my ear and I couldn't even make out what she was saying. She was so excited. Finally I heard her say, "Oh my gosh! Read the letter to me!"

I picked up the letter from the kitchen table and read it slowly to Jane. She was completely silent and most likely crying. I finished and said, "Well, what should I do now?"

"Read it again!"

I laughed and did as she asked. Then I said, "I meant...what should I do now that we know it is her?"

"When did she mail the letter?"

"Well, the letter was written and stamped June 29. Ellen said it arrived just a couple days after I left. She has been dying for me to get home."

Jane then said, "Oh my, Leona probably wonders why you haven't contacted her and never answered her calls. You have to call her tonight. It will still be early in California."

"Yes, I think you are right. I will give her a call. I will call you back after I talk to her. I think I will call Jan first though."

"Okay, that sounds great! Congratulations! You did a super job and Mother will be so excited. Wish I could be there when you tell her. Oh my!"

After hanging up from talking to Jane, I called my other sister, Janice, whom we call Jan. I had only told Ellen and just recently Jane about my search so I knew this was going to be a shocker to her. I dialed her number and she answered. "Hello?"

"Hi, Jan, how are you doing?"

"Well hi, this is a pleasant surprise," she said. "Did you make it home from Florida? How was your trip?"

"Oh, it was great as always. We had a wonderful time. How is all in Texas? As hot there as it is here?" I asked.

"It has been miserable. Great day to just stay inside. I have been working a little bit to get ready for school (she was a school speech pathologist). It will be here before we know it. I am sure you have enjoyed your first summer break."

"Yep, it has been nice. This summer is one to remember for sure. Are you sitting down? If not, you need to sit down. It is good news though," I said with a chuckle so not to worry her too much.

"Really? Okay, I'm sitting. What's up?"

"Well, I have some surprising news. Over spring break I started to do a little research for my third graders about the history of Kansas and Topeka. I went to the state historical society and got some great information, but while I was there I learned about the microfiche with all the state census information. Well, remember how Mother gave us all copies of her adoption papers at Christmas?"

"Oh yes, I read them over and found them very interesting."

"Okay, so I got to thinking when I was at the historical society, what if Mother's birth mother was from Kansas rather than Missouri? Mother always just assumed she was from Missouri since she was born there. So I started searching through the files county by county for a Leona Hendrickson. Well, long story short, I found her."

There was a long pause. Jan said, "What? No way! Tell me everything!"

I proceeded to fill her in about my search at the historical society, my conversations with Bus Wade and Leona's cousin Claude, and then the letters. She was so excited and totally astonished. I gave her all the details and read the letter to her. I told her I had finally shared with Jane when I was in Florida and had not said anything before to not get anyone's hopes up.

"I just called Jane and she was so excited. She said I should call Leona right now. I told her I would call and tell you first then call Leona since she said to call her later in the evening and it's still pretty early there."

"Wow, I am just shocked. And how are you going to tell Mother?" she asked and laughed at same time. "I wish I could be there for that."

I laughed, "Yeah, that's what Jane said. I haven't thought through that yet. It will be a shock for sure."

"Okay, well call me back after you talk to Leona. I want all the details. This is really cool. Talk to you soon. Love you."

We hung up and I sat down thinking through the questions I wanted to ask Leona. I jotted some of them down on a piece of paper. In Leona's letter she had said to call around 9:00 at night but that would be 11:00 my time. It sounded like she was a night owl just like my mother. However, there was no way I could wait that long. I decided to give it a try and call her earlier. It was about 8:30 my time so it would be about 6:30 in California. Hopefully she would be finished with supper and I wouldn't be disturbing her watching "Wheel of Fortune" like my mother did religiously each night at 6:30. We all knew best not to call home during her favorite TV shows.

Before I called Leona, it dawned on me that I should tape the conversation. Didn't even register that it was probably as illegal as the Watergate taping. I set up my tape recorder next to the speaker on my phone. I picked up the receiver and punched the numbers. Ring, ring, ring.

Chapter 16

After the third ring, someone picked up. A very sweet voice said, "Hello?"

"Is this Mrs. Bretches?" I asked.

"Yes, I am."

"Hi, this is KelLee Parr calling from Topeka, Kansas. How are doing tonight?"

"Just fine. How are you?"

"Just fine. Thank you so much for your letter!"

"Well, I was beginning to wonder if you had gotten it or not."

"Oh no, I was afraid of that. I've been visiting my sister in Florida. I left July 1st and didn't get back until the 15th, just today."

"Well, I was just sittin' reading the paper and it crossed my mind. I've just been sittin' here wondering."

"I'm so excited to finally get to talk to you. I imagine it was quite a surprise to get my letter."

"It was really a shock you might say," Leona said with a nervous laugh. "I hadn't heard anything for so long. I was really glad to get it."

"Good, I'm glad you were. It is one of those things; you don't want to interrupt anyone's life." I continued, "Like I said in the letter, my mother was always very interested in trying to locate you. It's just unbelievable how it's all worked out since I started to look."

"I am so happy you did!" Leona said in a thankful voice. "I couldn't decide whether to write or not. It was just something never talked about. In them days, it was terrible if something like that happened to you and so you tried to keep it to yourself or away from everybody else. But now days they don't think anything about it."

"Yes, that must have been a difficult time," I said.

"I tried calling you but never left a message when you didn't answer. I was thinking maybe you had changed your mind and didn't want to talk to this old country hick. I know I don't write very well," she laughed nervously.

"No, no, no, I'm so sorry for that. Your letter was great. I had been so excited to get home and see if I'd heard back from you."

I went on to tell her about my search and how I had located her using the adoption papers. I shared about Bus Wade and talking to her cousin Claude. I mentioned that I had noticed from her letter that her cousin gave me the wrong spelling of her name. I told her I tried calling information to get her phone number but there was no listing for that name. She laughed and said her cousin always spelled her name wrong, spelling it "Britches" with an "i" instead of an "e." But her phone number wasn't listed under her name anyway, it was listed under R. J. Bretches, her husband's name.

With a smile in her voice she said, "How is your mother? Is she okay?"

"Oh yes, she is doing great. She is going to be so happy to know I found you. She probably will want to get on the first plane and fly out to meet you."

"That would be just fine," Leona chuckled. "I would meet her at the airport."

"My mother gets very emotional and I know she will cry when I tell her about you."

"I don't have very many tears anymore," Leona said. "I have lost them all. It hurts on the inside but I never cry." She went on to say chuckling, "And if I get mad enough, I cuss instead of cry.

Sometimes that works just as well. It don't help any, but it makes me feel better I think. But it don't happen often."

We both laughed and knew I was going to love this lady.

"I can't wait to know more about you and your mother. Giving up your mother was the hardest thing I've ever done in my life. I honestly didn't know what to do when I got your letter. I was pretty shocked when I opened and read it asking if I was your grandmother and your mother's birth mother. I never thought anyone would ever ask me about that time of my life. I sort of squelched it all these years and never talked about her to anyone. It's been my secret all these years."

I said. "Please know we don't mean to interfere or make things uncomfortable for you. Like I said, my mother just always wanted to find you and know more about you."

Leona went on and shared, "After reading your letter the first time, for several days I pondered over what to do and reread your letter a dozen times. I was thrilled and scared at the same time. I still couldn't decide what to do. I never ever thought I would know what had happened to Marcia. I had to promise that I would never ever try and find or contact her."

She paused as a new thought popped into her head and continued, "Oh, you didn't say your mother's name in your letter. I've wondered if she's still called Marcia."

"My grandparents renamed her Wanda June."

"Wanda June. All these years she's always been my baby Marcia. I have dreamed about her and the life she had."

"As I shared in my letter, I am happy to tell you she had wonderful parents and has had a great life."

"That makes me so very happy to know," Leona hesitated to regain a little composure. "Like I was saying, I made that promise and kept it a secret all these years and your letter threw me for a spin. I didn't know if this would be breaking that promise. When I left the girls' home, I went to my sister Iva's who was married with kids and living in Garnett, Kansas. Iva just passed away this year on February 29. She was 91 years old on February 15, the day after Marcia's birthday."

"Oh I am so sorry."

"Iva's daughter, Lola, still lives in Garnett and I am very close to her and we stay in touch."

"I know where Garnett is. My parents have good friends that live there."

"So after a couple days of stewing over what to do, I called Lola," Leona said. "I read her your letter and asked her what she thought and whether I should write you back. Lola was stunned. She actually didn't know that I'd had a baby. She remembered when I came and stayed with them, but she was very young and just thought Aunt Leona had come to visit them for a while. My sister never told Lola that I had a baby. I sort of figured Iva had told her. But it was something that nobody in my family ever talked about, and we have kept it a secret all these years."

"Wow that was a big secret and a big surprise for your niece for certain. What did she say?" I asked.

"She was very sweet. Lola didn't even hesitate and told me 'Aunt Leona, they have reached out to you and you need to share with them about yourself because you're a sweet and special lady. You deserve to know about your daughter and grandchildren. Absolutely I think you should write them back. I'm really shocked by the news and can't believe you have a daughter and more family, but I'm so happy for you and think this is wonderful. It is amazing they found you.'"

Leona added, "So I sat down and wrote you that letter. It took me a couple tries, I was so nervous and shaky. I hope you could read my horrible handwriting. I don't write many letters anymore. And my grammar and spelling are terrible."

I had to laugh and said, "Your handwriting was just fine. My mother must have gotten her spelling skills from you because we've always teased her about what a bad speller she is. Your letter was perfect. I've read it several times. I even called both of my sisters to tell them the news and read your letter to them."

"Oh my, you mentioned in your letter that you have two sisters. Please tell me more about your mother and your family."

I retold Leona what I had shared in the letter with more detail about my mother. She had been adopted by Lynn and Emma Keller from Delia, Kansas. They had four other children. The two oldest were boys named Phil, who also was adopted, and John Vernon. The younger daughters were Naomi, just a year younger than my mother, and Geneva. Grandma Keller got pregnant almost immediately each time after bringing her newly adopted babies home.

I shared that my mother married my dad, Leroy "Lee" Parr in 1946. "Dad still farms and Mother used to work in Topeka but she is semi-retired now. She worked as a registered orthopedic technologist helping fit braces on people needing back, arm and leg braces. Now she works part-time as a receptionist for an eye doctor in Rossville."

"What a wonderful thing for her to have done, helping people," Leona interjected with pride in her voice.

"Of course Mother also has helped on the farm. I think I told you in the letter that they live on the farm where she grew up. She can drive the tractor and combine with the best of the guys. She grew up a real country girl and loved being outdoors and loved to hunt and fish. I found it so interesting that you said in your letter that you loved to hunt and fish too."

"Oh yes, my husband and I loved to hunt and fish together," Leona added. She was tickled pink that she and her daughter had this in common.

"Dad and Mother have us three children. I have one sister named Jane who lives in Florida. She is 43 and not married. Janice is just about to turn 40 and lives in Arlington, Texas. She is married and her husband's name is Louie. Her last name is Nash. They have two children. Bo is thirteen and Elizabeth or EJ, which stands for Elizabeth Jane, is in fourth grade and is nine. I am the youngest and not married and teach school."

"Oh my, that's wonderful," she laughed, almost seeming overwhelmed.

"Do you have other children?" I asked.

"Yes and no," she chuckled that little laugh I came to love. "I met Russell Bretches when I was 19 years old back in Kansas. He was wonderful to me and I fell in love with the tall, good-looking man. I was scared to tell him that I'd had a baby out of wedlock. But when I told him, he didn't even bat an eye. He said he loved me for me and wanted to marry me. I told him having to give up my baby Marcia was the hardest thing I ever had to do. And if I couldn't have her, I didn't want to have any children. Russell said, 'Ona, if that's what you want, then that's just fine by me.' So we never did have kids."

"So, what did you mean then when you said 'yes and no'?" I asked.

"Well, it's kind of a long story but after we got married, we moved to Portland, Oregon, to find work. It was such a hard time to find work back home in those days. My brother Louis moved out here to find work because we couldn't keep the farm going during the Depression. He wrote me and Russell and told us he had found work and was helping to build roads up to Crater Lake. He said it was pretty hard work but if we came out we both could get a job and 'make pretty good money for those times. At first we just lived out of a tent. It was a rough life and no place for kids."

"That's incredible. It must have been quite an adventure."

"Yes, it was and one of my favorite times in my life. Things were tough but so much simpler. It was so beautiful working in those mountains and the beautiful forests. We just loved it, but it was back-breaking work and the winters were really rough."

"One day in 1944 we got word that my sister Goldie was very sick. She still lived in Kansas and was married with two children,

Darlene and Orville. We headed back to Kansas as soon as we could, but we didn't get home before Goldie passed away. Her husband, Ernest, tried to take care of Goldie's babies and wasn't able to do a very good job. Darlene was thirteen and Orville was almost six. He wasn't ready to raise a teenage girl and small boy all alone. Mama wanted to help but she was getting too old to take care of them. I told Russell that I thought we should take Goldie's kids home with us and raise them. He just smiled at me and said, 'Ona, whatever you want.'"

"Russell sounds like he was a great guy," I said.

"Yes, he was. I miss him so much. Russell and I went to Goldie's husband and said we wanted to bring the kids back with us. He agreed and we loaded them on the train with us, brought 'em back to Oregon, and raised 'em as our own. We bought a little house in Klamath Falls. That was my first house after all those years living in a tent, and then a little silver Airstream trailer we bought after we made enough money."

She paused and I could tell she was getting a little emotional. "That must have been really wonderful to finally have your own house," I said.

"Yes, it made me very happy to live in town. So long story short, I raised my sister's children. Darlene is married to Joe and they live on a ranch with their son, Geren. They had a son Donald who drowned and daughter Barbara was killed when a horse kicked her. Joe has multiple sclerosis now, and Darlene has had a rough go of things."

"Oh my, that's very sad."

"My Orville and his wife, Betty, have two boys, Russell and Louis. They were named after my husband and brother. Betty has a daughter, Julia, from a previous marriage. They all call me Aunt Leona but they're more like my grandchildren to me."

We continued to talk for what turned out to be a forty-five minute, uninterrupted exchange of our lives. It was incredible to learn so much about a person that until this moment had only been someone we imagined.

I told Leona that I hadn't told my mother yet. "I didn't tell my mother that I was looking for you. And once I found your name and talked to your cousin, I didn't want to get her hopes up in case I was going down the wrong trail. Are you okay with me telling her now?"

Without hesitation she said "Yes, please do! She is going to be as shocked as I was I bet. I would love to see her face when you tell her."

I laughed and said, "You know you're the third person to say that to me today. Like I said, I bet she is going to want to come see you if she can. I don't know what her work schedule is like or if she can get away, but I know she will want to do so."

"Well, that would be just fine," Leona said and hesitated before saying, "I am not crazy about everybody here in Dorris knowing about it. But if your mother wants to come out, I'll say she is my cousin or something like that while she is here," she laughed. "But I sure would like to see her."

I'm going to go out to the farm tomorrow and tell her. How about I give you a call tomorrow evening and you can talk to her?"

"Oh my," Leona said. "I don't know that she'll want to talk to this old thing."

"I guarantee you she will want to talk to you and will be so happy to hear your voice. What's a good time for us to give you a call? I know you said in your letter after 9:00 at night was a good time to call. Sounds like you stay up late. My mother burns the midnight oil and stays up late too."

"Yes, Russell always said I was his night owl."

"Would it be okay if we called you earlier, maybe in the late afternoon? I'll be going out to the farm. My mother should be home around 5:00. I'll tell her the news and then maybe we could call you. There's a two hour difference in our time so how about we call you at 4:00 your time? Is that a good time for you?"

"Oh yes, I'll be here," she said. "Thank you so much for finding me. You have no idea how much this means to me."

"You're very welcome and you have no idea how much this means to all of us as well. Thank you and we will call you tomorrow at 4:00. I can't wait to tell my mother and to learn more about you and your family. Goodbye."

"Bye."

I sat in utter disbelief. Did that conversation just really happen? Yes, it did. I had just talked to my long lost grandmother.

Chapter 17

That evening I was on the phone with both of my sisters for several hours sharing my conversation with Leona. Also there was the call to my parents to let them know I had made it home safely from Florida. Of course I had hoped my dad would answer the phone and I would just tell him I was home safely and that I would be coming to the farm the next day and talk then. The chance of him ever answering the phone was slim to none since Mother's chair was parked right next to the phone. By the time I got around to calling them, Dad was in bed anyway.

My mother answered, "Well, about time I heard from you. I was wondering if you got back from Jane's okay."

"Yep, made it just fine. Sorry to call so late but just got busy talking to Ellen next door and unpacking. I had to call Jane and let her know I made it home okay, too. I figured you guys would be out working 'til dark anyway," avoiding the real reason I had not called earlier.

We chitchatted about my trip and all that had gone on at the farm while I was away. There was no mention of Leona to my mother, of course. No way was I going to drop this bombshell over the phone. I told her I would see her out at the farm the next day. She reminded me that she was going to be working at the eye doctor's office in Rossville. I told her I would stop by there on my way to the farm but it probably would be afternoon before I headed that way. We said our goodbyes and hung up.

It was hard to get to sleep that night as I replayed the conversation with Leona over and over. I was trying to figure out how I was going to break the news to my mother that I had found the piece to the puzzle she had always been seeking.

The next morning I woke up early, especially from still being on Florida time. I puttered around my condo unpacking and getting things cleaned up after being away for a couple of weeks. I needed to pay bills and run out to the school district to pick up my summer check. After lunch I ran a few more errands then headed back to my condo. I gathered my notes, Leona's letters, and the cassette tape of our conversation and headed to the farm.

Chapter 18

Rossville is the little town of about 1000 residents where my sisters and I went to high school. It was a pleasant twenty-minute drive from Topeka to Rossville. My dad grew up on a farm three miles outside of Rossville, and our family had lived there near my Grandpa and Grandma Parr until I was 12 years old. Then we moved to the farm where my mother grew up, which was about 14 miles north of Rossville and almost seven miles to the tiny town of Delia.

Delia had a population of about 300 people, dogs and cats. Not sure which there were more of though. At the time we moved to my Grandpa Keller's farm in 1968, Delia still had a small K–8 grade school with two grades per classroom. I was in the seventh grade when we moved. All the older kids went to Rossville High School so my sister avoided the misfortune of switching schools.

As I went through Rossville on my way to the farm, I stopped at the optometrist's office to see my mother. I drove into town from the south after being slowed down by the big S curves that no one could ever explain why the road wasn't built straight. I passed the little park with the big cement statue of a lion guarding the entrance. Highway 24, a major two-lane road, cuts through the middle of town east and west running parallel next to the Union Pacific Railroad. Once you stop at the only stoplight in town at the highway intersection and cross over the railroad tracks, you have reached downtown Rossville and Main Street.

Rossville was your typical rural Kansas small town. The downtown hadn't changed much over the years except for the new bank. The old library was gone and moved into the old bank building on the other end of Main Street. There was Wehner's IGA grocery store on the right and the Rossville Truck and Tractor on the left. My dad spent many an hour in that building telling stories with the other farmers and the owners, Bill and George. At the end of downtown was the intersection where everyone dragging Main Street on a Friday night would make the big U-turn and head back for another trip. The optometrist's office was just to the left of the intersection next to the new laundromat.

I parked and got out to visit my mother. I was nervous. I knew I couldn't say anything to her now about Leona, or she would be a mess trying to work the rest of the afternoon. So I planned to just stop and say "Hi" and let her see for herself that I had made it home safely from Florida.

Mother was all alone in the office as both optometrists were away and no customers were in the office. We chatted and I asked her how everything was going. She said everything was fine but she was really getting tired of working and had told Dr. Carriger that morning she would only act as a temporary after they found someone to replace her.

It was kind of surprising to hear her say she was wanting to quit as I knew she really enjoyed working there. I asked her what she thought she would do to stay busy. She said, "Well, your dad is slowing down too, and we want to travel and go see the girls and Bo and EJ more."

"They all would love that if you went to see them. Jane was just saying how she hoped you could come down to visit," I told her.

"Another thing I told Doctor C. is that I want to take some time and try and do some research to see if I could find more information about my birth mother. I was watching Oprah the other day and she had a show with people that had found their birth parents. It was so inspirational. They told how they went about finding their birth parents. It got me motivated to start looking again to see if I can find anything out about my birth mother or any other family that might be out there."

After pulling my jaw up off the floor, I gathered my thoughts and nonchalantly told her, "I think that's a wonderful idea. I know how badly you've always wanted to find something out about your birth mother."

"Yes, I have been thinking about this a lot lately since your grandpa passed away. I always was a little hesitant to search too hard not wanting to hurt Mom and Dad's feelings or for them to think I didn't love or appreciate them."

Grandma Keller passed away in 1980 at 90 years old after many years in a nursing home, suffering from Alzheimer's. Grandpa Keller remained in his Rossville home living alone until he moved into the nursing home just a few months before his 100th birthday, December 19, 1990. In typical Lynn Keller fashion, his death that year on New Years' Eve was almost seemed planned. He made his goal of reaching 100 and made things easy for his kids for taking care of his estate by not starting a new tax year.

Mother went on to say, "I've thought more about it and figure I better get to looking while I still can. I never have really had time to devote much effort searching and this show really got me encouraged to get started again. I don't imagine my birth mother is still alive but I would love to find out anything I can."

Just then a gal from my high school days and her daughter came in the doctor's office. The little girl needed her glasses adjusted. Talk about relieved to be able to change the subject. We all chatted a bit then I said, "I better let you get those glasses fixed and I'll go see how Dad's doing out at the farm and if there's anything I can help him with this afternoon. It was great to see you. And Mother, I'll see you when you get home. Bye."

"Bye!"

Wow, how crazy was that? I couldn't believe my mother just said she was going to start looking for her birth mother again. Little did she know....

Pulling away from the eye doctor's office, I headed my silver Mazda truck toward Main Street and turned north. Each house I passed in the four blocks of houses, I thought of a cousin, classmate, or family friend that lived or had lived in each house. It is one of the wonderful things about small towns. It is like one large family and everybody knows everybody.

I went by my cousin Anita's house on the left, then Aunt Naomi's house on the right, and a couple houses down I could see my Uncle Vernon's house on the left. I smiled thinking how lucky my mother and all of us were to have such a great family and now our family had just gotten bigger. I wondered how my mother's family would react when they found out the news about finding Leona.

Chapter 19

It was a beautiful summer day and I enjoyed the final leg of my trip to the farm. Once reaching Delia, the two-lane, paved road becomes gravel and the dust began to fly. I loved driving on these old gravel roads. The only thing I didn't like was the coating of dust my pickup would have after my return trip home.

As I was going along, Don Miller passed me in his old pickup truck and waved. It didn't matter if people in the country knew you or not, they were going to wave. I loved how friendly these people were. It reminded me of Bus Wade. I thought, "I bet he waved at everybody going down the country roads of Havana."

The Keller/Parr farm was located on the edge of the rolling Flint Hills and on the Potawatomi Indian Reservation. My parents moved to this farm in 1968 after my Grandma Keller became ill with what they incorrectly referred to as "hardening of the arteries." She had dementia, which was probably Alzheimer's disease, as it is now known. My grandmother became very confused and would wander off. My cousin Skip's wife Karen stayed with Grandpa and Grandma while Skip was in the Navy, but the day came when the difficult decision was made to move off the farm.

It was very comforting to my grandpa when my parents said they were interested in moving from Rossville and taking over the farm. My mother shared that as a little girl she would ride her pony and carry drinking water to her dad and brothers working in the fields. Every day on her little pony she prayed that one day she would get to live on their farm when she was older. So her prayers came true. Sadly, thirty short years later, my parents had to move off the same farm because my dad also developed Alzheimer's.

As I traveled the last two miles, I saw our farmhouse and outbuildings in the distance. There was nothing between me and the farm but pasture, trees, and the large pond where we used to fish and ice skate. My parents took such pride in keeping the farm looking nice, and we kids were always proud to bring friends from college out to the farm because it was so beautiful. Of course our friends also were afraid they might never find their way back to school because we were so far out in the "boonies," as my dad would call it. In fact, Jan was a senior in high school when we moved, and she lamented how she would never have a date again because none of the boys would want to drive so far out in the middle of nowhere to get her. Though with dates to three different proms her senior year, I guess that was a moot issue.

Rounding the final corner to drive the last quarter-mile north to the house, I had one last steep hill to traverse down. All of us grandkids thought this was the best hill in the world for sledding as long as you didn't veer off into the creek at the bottom of the hill. From the hilltop I could see the large red barn that used to be filled with hay clear to the silver tin roof. What a great place we had! We could build forts, swing from ropes, and play "Hide and Go Seek." The old barn sat empty once Dad started baling the big round bales.

I saw the white fences that encircled the farm and the big open driveway that doubled as the baseball field. There was the white granary with the brown wood shingle roof where we all played "Annie, Annie Over," throwing the ball over the roof and if caught, the catching team ran around trying to tag members of the throwing team.

The huge silver machine shed and hay barn were surrounded by the empty cattle feedlots Dad was cleaning. He used the tractor and loader to scoop up the manure, load the manure spreader, and haul it down to the fields to fertilize next year's grain crop. Dad was on his tractor when I pulled up, and I knew he would have seen the dust flying as I came down the hill.

There were two huge silver poles on either side of the entrance to the driveway with another huge silver pole across the top connecting the two upright poles. Centered and welded to the top bar were the individual letters, about one foot by two foot that spelled the name PARR. My mother painted the poles silver and our last name bright red. There were two white wooden signs hanging side-by-side from chains and iron brackets painted black. The "hello" side of the signs read "Flying P Farm" and "Lee and Wanda Parr." The "goodbye" signs read "Glad you came" and "Come back again."

My mother designed the entrance way and asked George Olejnik, the blacksmith in Delia, to make this as a surprise Father's Day present for my dad. It was a huge project and pain in the butt for my dad to get "his" present erected.

Huge holes had to be dug. Dad had to ask some neighbors for help, and it took a couple tractors with loaders to sink the poles into the rocky Kansas earth. Once the poles were in, they poured cement in the holes and staked them to make sure they were level and didn't move until the cement was set. There were plenty of choice words while my mother gave directions and the neighbors chuckled about my dad's Father's Day "present." We all knew who the entrance way was really for, though all said and done, my dad was very proud of it and like he said, "It isn't going anywhere any time soon."

The PARR sign still stands at the farm though the Potawatomi Indian tribe bought the house when my parents moved to town because of my dad's Alzheimer's disease. The tribe used the house for a rehabilitation center. Creatively, they put up a sign in the yard: "PARR– Potawatomi Alcohol Rehabilitation Residence."

Chapter 20

I pulled in and parked in front of the beautiful white farmhouse. My parents' house was originally a four-room, little house that my grandparents moved into when they bought the farm. The house had been added on to several times in every conceivable way. The wrap-around porch my grandparents added had long been divided into additional rooms including a sunroom where Dad would sit and watch baseball games on TV while keeping an eye out on the farmyard, much the way Grandpa Parr had done on his farm.

The normally pristine yard was covered with boards and saw horses. My cousin, Randy, a master carpenter, was transforming the remaining porch into an additional sitting area that expanded the formal dining room. A new deck was being added to the front as well.

Randy was Aunt Naomi's oldest child. He and my cousin Mick worked for my parents all through high school during the summers. Randy worked for a couple years after graduating before starting his carpentry career. Randy was also adopted and held a special place in my mother's heart. It was interesting that both Aunt Naomi and Aunt Geneva had each adopted a child.

My mother and Randy would banter back and forth, teasing one another about anything and everything. It was great fun listening to them give each other a hard time. Mother was a pretty good carpenter herself. Though she had no design training, she had great ideas and wanted them executed to her high level of expectation. This led to many interesting "disagreements" during the remodeling projects.

When my parents first moved to the farm, my mother wanted the whole house remodeled and knew exactly what she wanted. She met with George "Boob" Murback, a retired carpenter friend of Grandpa Keller's that lived close by. I never knew how he got that nickname, but he was a delightful and intelligent man. Wanda convinced Boob to help her to do the remodeling. With Mother's vision and Boob's meticulous carpentry skills, they created some masterful woodworking.

Together, they built beautiful kitchen cabinets, a built-in china hutch, several corner bookshelves, and other cabinets that utilized every nook and cranny in that house. When you walked in the front door, there was a hallway that led to the kitchen area. On the left side from floor to ceiling were three sets of wooden doors. There were three bottom doors that were about five feet tall and two feet wide. The top doors were about three feet tall. Behind all the doors but one were little shelves about the depth of canned goods. This was Mother's pantry. The last door didn't have shelves and was for her mops and brooms. All her design. Her pantry was the envy of all the neighbors.

Boob and Wanda went round and round during all the construction and almost daily he would say, "Lady, we can't do that," or "you crazy lady," but they had a fabulous time working together. After the remodeling was done, he told her he had to admit she had been right most of the time and was so proud of their work.

So when Randy started working on the dining room and deck, his Aunt Wanda again definitely had her ideas of how things should be done. She expressed to Randy how he should do something and made no bones about it. Randy had no trouble giving it right back to her and would do the job his way, the right way. My dad and I laughed because it was a repeat performance from the Boob and Wanda Show.

As I was getting out of my truck, I saw my dad on his tractor come around the hay shed towards the house. I knew he would stop to say hello so I was running though my head whether to tell him about Leona or wait until my mother got home. He drove the tractor pulling the loaded manure spreader to a stop in front of the red barn and climbed down and waved.

As Dad approached the sidewalk, he said "Hi, welcome home" and asked me to pump some water to wash his dirty hands. There was an old hand water pump in front of the house that had a long pipe leading down off the cement platform. We all loved taking turns pumping water from the old well when we were grandkids. I gave the old black handle a few pumps and water slowly rose up from the well in the center pipe. The water came out, running down the long extended pipe. Dad reached down and washed his hands with the cool water and doused his face. "Now that feels good," he said then wiped his hands on the towel that always hung on the wooden fence post next to the cement platform.

He came up onto the cement platform and we both sat down on the front steps leading up to the house. He asked me how my trip to Florida was and how my sister Jane was doing. I told him about my trip and he shared that nothing much new had happened on the farm. A couple days had been real scorchers while I was gone and they had a little rain but still needed more. As typical for a farmer, the weather was the most important factor.

I decided I needed to let Dad in on my news. "I stopped at Rossville and saw Mother on my way out to the farm. She tells me she's decided to stop working."

"Yes, she has wanted to do that for some time," he said.

"She mentioned to me she was wanting to start doing more research to try to find information about her birth mother."

He smiled and said, "Yes, she's wanted to know about her mother as long as I've known her. That's the one thing that has always bugged her and she really would like to know more about her background. She watched an Oprah show about adopted kids finding their folks and that got her all fired up, I think."

"Yeah, she was telling me about that. That's kind of interesting because I might be able to help her with that."

Dad gave me this funny glance and that "go on" look.

"Do you remember Mother gave each of us kids copies of her adoption papers last Christmas? That had some information about where Mother was born and her birth name was Marcia Hendrickson and her mother's name was Leona May. We always thought she was from Missouri because she was born in Kansas City. Well, I was doing some research for my lessons for my class at the Kansas Historical Society and found out how to look up people in the old state census reports. I got to thinking, what if Leona was from Kansas and her name was on one of these old censuses?"

"That's a good thought," Dad said. "You'll have to tell your mom about that."

"Well, I don't think I need to do that, Dad. What would you say if I told you I found her birth mother? And what's more, I spoke to Leona on the phone last night."

The look on my dad's face was one of amazed confusion. He was trying to process it. "You what? How?"

I went on to explain all that had transpired over the past few months. Repeating the story I had told my sisters, I shared about Bus Wade, cousin Claude, and the letter I wrote to Leona, how she wrote me back and I had called and talked to her last night. He was speechless and I noticed he had a little tear in the corner of his eye.

After I had finished with the background of finding Leona, I asked him what he thought.

"This is amazing. You have just made your mother's dream come true and she will be so happy. So tell me about your conversation with Leona on the phone."

"That was very cool. She sounded like a very sweet lady and was pretty nervous but excited I had contacted her. I taped the conversation so you can listen to it if you want."

"I'll wait until your mom gets home and listen to it then. Did you tell her when you saw her in Rossville?"

"No way. I figured she better be home and not having to try and work when she gets this bombshell. You know she will be a crying mess."

He laughed and said that was smart thinking. I told him I had told Jane and Jan and that Ellen had been my co-conspirator, no one else knew yet. We sat and talked for a little more. He said Randy had already finished and gone home for the day then added, "Well, this manure isn't going to spread itself and I had better get back to work and try and get one more load hauled before supper."

"I'll fix some supper before Mother gets home and set things up to share the news. After all these years, it is finally happening for her."

My dad was not a hugger but before he stood he slapped me on the knee, winked and said, "This is wonderful news. I want to be here when she finds out."

Chapter 21

Dad got a drink of water and headed back to his tractor. I went into the house and saw my mother's tape player on the kitchen table where it could usually be found. She loved to make cassette tape letters to send to people. She also would listen to books on tape or music while cooking or when there wasn't anything good on TV. I put my tape in the player to share Leona's and my phone conversation from the night before. Entering the kitchen to figure out what to fix for supper, I checked the fridge and noted some fresh tomatoes and onions. We always had some of Dad's home-grown beef available and there was some hamburger thawed in the meat drawer. I decided to fix Mother's favorite goulash recipe for supper.

My mother was an excellent cook and made sure we all learned as well, though some of us were better cooks than others. Before my sisters went off to college, they worked out an agreement quite suitable to all of us that Jan cooked and Jane cleaned. I loved cooking in my mother's kitchen. Mother designed the kitchen herself much to Boob's disgruntlement. Despite all the renovations and improvements, it was really only big enough for one person, two at the most. Boob thought she was crazy—who had such a dinky kitchen? She designed her kitchen this way because her previous kitchen at our old house was huge and she hated having to walk across from sink to stove to the fridge. "I don't like other people in my kitchen and this keeps them out," she always said laughing.

The kitchen was a U-shape with a sink at the bottom of the "U" and a window that looked out to the sunroom. She would proudly say, "This allows me to wash my dishes, talk to Lee in the sunroom, and look out at the farm all at the same time." Each side had counters and floor-to-ceiling wood cabinets she had designed with Boob's help when we first moved into the house. It was amazing the storage space they had created.

A Corning Cooktop stove was on one side of the "U" and the microwave and dutch ovens on the other. One could take a pan out of the oven and put it on the stove with no more than a turn and tiny step. It was efficiency at its best. Her first ever dishwasher was next to the ovens and the width of the kitchen was just wide enough to open the dishwasher door all the way.

At the top of the U-shaped kitchen was the fridge on one side and then next a long counter that almost closed the top of the "U" and buffered direct access to the kitchen. The counter was built especially with making her famous peanut brittle in mind. Many a day leading up to Christmas she poured her peanut brittle fresh off the stove onto the buttered counter top, and we all would use forks to stretch the brittle out thin, filling the space completely.

A few minutes before 5:00 p.m., a familiar noise jarred me from prepping for supper and my thoughts of what to say to break the news. Mother had just pulled into the garage. She had to climb the stairs, which was an add-on to the original old farmhouse. At one point my grandfather had added two more bedrooms to the house and put a basement under that portion of the house. The garage was on the same level as the basement so my mother had to climb the eight or nine steps up to the main floor of the house and then down the hallway to the small kitchen on the left.

The goulash simmered in the electric skillet and the familiar aroma permeated the house. Mother came into the kitchen just as I was buttering garlic bread to put in the oven, and she gave me a hug. "That smells wonderful. Are you making goulash? I'm starving."

"Yes, I thought it sounded good. I know how much you like it."

Dad followed my mother up the stairs, carrying in her groceries. No Parr went to town without bringing home groceries because we lived so far out in the sticks. He set the brown paper bags from Wehner's grocery store on the counter and gave me another quick wink when my Mother wasn't looking. You would never have known we had a secret from the expressions on our faces. Dad went and washed up and headed to "his" recliner in the sunroom to await my mother's reaction to the news.

My mother and I put the groceries away and I told her we had some time before supper would be ready. Actually the goulash had just started cooking and I knew we had lots of time. I didn't think Dad or I could sit all the way through supper without telling her about Leona. I turned the skillet control so it would cook slowly.

My mother sat down in "her" black leather, high-backed chair adjacent to the counter that blocked off her kitchen. She had a perfect line of sight to the little TV on the built-in cupboard sitting catty-cornered from the kitchen table. She was just steps from the kitchen and could reach the phone as well. The wall phone had a cord that would stretch about 10 feet so she could also be in the kitchen working and talking at the same time. There was a little chalkboard next to the wall phone where we always left messages. Next to the chalkboard was a little cork board with newspaper clippings of special interest pinned to the board. These were the articles cut out of newspapers and magazines she planned to send to friends and family. This must have been genetic because later we discovered Leona did the same thing.

I sat down at the kitchen table, and we started to chat. I told her about Florida and filled her in on all the details we didn't get to at the optometrist's office. I complimented Randy's progress on the remodeling project. Truthfully, the new formal dining room looked like a disaster area after he had ripped off the old porch and tore down the exterior wall. My mother said, "Randy is doing a great job. He's such a good kid and is meticulous with his work. I don't know how he remembers all the measurements without writing them down. Just amazes me. I imagine he was probably glad I was working today and not here to boss him around."

I laughed and agreed.

"Let's look at what he has done today," she said.

We walked to the new formal dining room area where we had to peel back the plastic barrier hanging from the archway to step into the area being remodeled. The plastic had been tacked up to keep the dust from coating the rest of the house.

My mother was a meticulous housekeeper and she said, "I will be so happy when this project is completed. I can't wait to get my house back to normal. The dust on everything is driving me crazy. But it is going to be so nice to have this larger room and the deck. You know this is something I have wanted done for a long time. The larger dining room will be so nice for all the family to sit around the table together."

My thought was, "Yes, and it is a good thing because your family has just gotten bigger."

Chapter 22

After looking over Randy's accomplishments, we were back at the kitchen table. This gave me a good opening, "Well now that you are getting your dining room done, what is another thing you have always wanted?" I asked.

After telling me earlier about quitting her job to look for her birth mother, I just knew that is what she would say. She paused and then said, "Hmmmm. I really want the old red barn painted."

I wanted to hit my head against the wall. I smiled and said, "That would be nice but surely there is something bigger than that you would like? Something you have always wanted?"

She hesitated and then quickly she said, "Oh, I think I told you I saw this show on Oprah about adopted children who had searched and found their birth parents. I told Dr. Carriger I wanted to stop working and spend some time looking for my birth mother. He suggested I check into getting a lawyer to see if I can't get the State of Missouri to give me more information since their records are sealed."

I looked at her and calmly said expressionless, "What would you say if I told you that you didn't need to do that?"

She stopped and looked at me with the funny stare like Arnold on the TV show *Different Strokes* when he would say, "What you talkin' about, Willis?"

I repeated my question again but this time with a little smile. She said, "What do you mean?"

"Well, what would you say if I told you that you don't have to do any searching," I said. "I found information about your birth mother?"

She screamed, "Oh my! No! What did you find?"

"Well, her name is Leona Bretches."

As mentioned before, my mother was a crier. It didn't matter if it was something sad, funny, or indifferent. If she heard good news of a friend's new baby, learned of the loss of someone's loved one (even if she had never heard of the person), or watched a movie (Gone with the Wind being her favorite), tears would be shed. It was a family joke that she should have made a Kleenex commercial. We knew to have tissues ready when any kind of news, happy or sad, was shared.

I was prepared that day and had placed tissues on the table ready to go. My mother didn't know what to say but just started to sob. I hadn't even had a chance to tell her any details. I got up and gave her a hug and asked if she wanted to know more? She nodded her head and barely audible said, "Please."

My next statement really opened the floodgates. "What would you say if I told you Leona is still alive and lives in California?"

"Oh KelLee. She's *alive*? I can't believe it!"

I started from the beginning, leaving out no detail. She responded with a constant river of tears and uncontrollable sobbing. When I finished telling her about the historical society, I could tell she needed a break. I got her a glass of water, and she took a few minutes to let it all soak in.

I shared with her about the sweet postmistress and Bus Wade from Havana, Kansas, and how he gave me information about the Hendricksons. How Bus had given me the phone number for Claude Hendrickson from Wichita and how I had contacted Claude asking about the Hendrickson family tree. He told me about his cousins, Leona and Bud, who lived in California. "Claude said he would give them my name and information to contact me, and I really had no idea if this was even the right

Leona or if either of them would contact me. But after a couple weeks, I got a letter from a Leona Bretches."

That's when I handed her the first letter I got from Leona. Mother held it shakily, tried to read it and then handed it back to me and asked me to read it to her. I read it slowly out loud and reread it again. Then she asked me to go on.

"After I heard back from Leona, I wrote her a letter telling her why I was looking for a Leona Hendrickson. I gave just enough information that if she was your birth mother, there would be no doubt it was her. I also said we didn't want to intrude in her life but that you had always wanted to find her. I mailed it and that is when I left for Florida."

The tears kept flowing.

"Did you hear from her again?" she sputtered between sobs.

"Well, Ellen collected my mail while I was gone and when I got back yesterday, there was another letter from Leona. And yes, she is your birth mother."

Huge sobs and tears were now almost uncontrollable. I was pretty teary eyed myself by this time and I know my dad was as well, even though he was sitting out in the sunroom listening. I patted her on the back. Some time passed and she gained a little composure, and I gave her a hug. She just stared at me as if almost in shock.

"I just can't believe this," she kept repeating.

"It's true. Would you like for me to read the letter to you?"

"Yes, please do," she said in a near whisper and wiped more tears.

As I read Leona's letter, my mother—the consummate crier—went off the charts.

> *I am writing this in regards to the letter I received from you. Have tried to call you but no answer. So I will write a few lines.*

Yes, I think I am the Leona May you are looking for. Sorry haven't written sooner. This was one subject that was never talked about but never forgotten.

Several times I had to stop to let my mother regain her composure to hear the words I was reading from her own mother. After finishing the letter, I gave it to her to hold and she began to read it very quietly to herself. As she held the letter in one hand and tissue in the other, her eyes danced across each line while sobbing. She wiped the tears of joy streaming down her beautiful face.

While she read, I checked on the goulash and it was almost done. I turned the heat down and peeked out the window that opened to the sunroom and winked at my dad. He was smiling from ear to ear, and I could tell he had been tearing up as well. He whispered chuckling, "Do you have enough Kleenexes?"

When I came back from the kitchen, my mother looked at me and said, "I can't believe I am reading my mother's handwriting. I have dreamed of this day for so long. I just can't believe it."

I nodded and said, "It's for real, it isn't a dream. One more thing, what would you say if I told you I spoke to her last night on the phone?"

"Oh my!!!!!!!!!!!"

More convulsions of joy.

I shared a little of our conversation and tears continued to stream as I told my mother what Leona had shared. Beaming, I had to be a little ornery, and I hesitated a bit and asked, "Would you like to hear her voice? I taped the conversation."

"No, you didn't. How did you do that?"

"I really don't know what made me think to do it but I put her on speaker phone and recorded our conversation. We can listen to it in a little bit. But better yet, she is waiting for us to call her this evening?"

"Really??? Tonight? She wants to talk to me?" More sobbing.

"Yes, I asked her last night if she would like to talk to you and that I was going to come out to the farm today to tell you. I told Leona I hadn't shared any of my search until I knew for sure she was your mother."

"Oh, what did she say?" Mother asked.

"She said she would love to talk to you and get to know you. She was very happy I had found her. We are to call her at 6:00 p.m. our time so we still have a little time to listen to some of the tape."

While she regained her composure, I went to the kitchen and made sure supper was doing okay and again looked out into the sunroom. Dad was just shaking his head and smiling still. I said, "We will be calling Leona in a little bit. Do you want to talk to her?"

"No, let your mom talk to her. This is her time."

Mother's tape recorder was on the kitchen table with the "Leona tape" cued up. We listened to a little of Leona's and my conversation and Mother was misty eyed the whole time. She just kept saying, "I can't believe this. I can't believe this. She sounds just like I had imagined. She sounds like such a nice lady."

Chapter 23

My mother was mesmerized, listening to her mother's voice and all she was sharing. Time went by very quickly. Right when my folks' big, wooden kitchen clock with the swinging pendulum sounded out six rings, I said it was time to call Leona. She looked at me almost in a panic. "Leona and I agreed that we would call her at 4:00 her time," I said.

Mother was so nervous it was cute. She said, "I don't know what to say."

She was never one to be without words and never knew a stranger. It was not uncommon for me to pick my mother up at the airport after a visit to one of my sisters and she would inevitably introduce me to the person she had sat next to on the plane. Obviously they had talked all the way on the plane and exchanged life stories, and on at least two of the trips, Mother had exchanged addresses with her new friends.

Mother sent out more than 300 Christmas cards with letters and handwritten notes every year. When her eyesight deteriorated, my sister started making mailing labels for all the people on her Christmas card list. Jan would call me and say, "Do you know who this is?" Neither of us had any idea who half of the people on the list were, so the joke became which flight Mother was on when she met this or that person who ended up on the coveted Christmas list.

"Just be yourself and don't worry," I said. "Leona's a sweet lady. I'm sure she's just as nervous as you. You will do just fine."

I went to the phone and dialed Leona's number. It rang as my mother stared anxiously, waiting to see if she was going to answer. The same sweet voice I heard on the phone last night said "Hello?"

"Hi Leona, this is KelLee. How are you tonight?"

"I am just fine. A bit nervous and didn't get much sleep last night," she laughed.

I chuckled back and said, "I understand. I didn't either. It was pretty exciting talking to you and hard to shut my mind down because of all the questions that came to me. I really enjoyed our chat."

"Oh, I did too. It was so nice to hear your voice and learn about my daughter."

"Well guess who I have standing here next to me?"

"Your mother, I am guessing," she said with more nervous laughter.

"Yes, and she's been crying tears of happiness ever since I told her just a little bit ago. She can't wait to talk to you, so I am going to put her on the phone if that's okay."

"Sure thing, I hope she isn't disappointed talking to this old thing."

I laughed and said, "Don't worry. She won't be at all."

I handed the phone receiver attached to the end of the long cord to my mother, sitting in her big leather chair. She looked at me and took a deep breath. She took the phone in one hand and again a fresh tissue in the other.

"Hello, is this Leona?" she asked.

"Yes, I am Leona May."

"How are you?"

"I am doing just fine. A little nervous but very excited to talk to you."

"Oh I am too. Are you really my mother?"

"Yes, honey, I'm your mother. I can't believe I am getting to talk to my baby girl Marcia."

"I can't believe it either. I am so happy you wanted to talk to me. I have dreamed of this moment all my life."

Leona and my mother must have talked for about 20 minutes; the conversation was pleasant and seemed to just flow easily. Leona told her a lot of what she shared with me the night before. Mother kicked into her naturally easy, conversational self and the tears stopped. At the end of the conversation, I heard my mother ask if it would be okay if she called Leona the next day and they could talk some more. Leona happily agreed.

"It was so nice to talk to you, Leona. I look forward to talking to you tomorrow. I will let you talk to KelLee again. Goodbye," Mother said and handed me the phone.

"Hi, sounds like you two are planning to talk again tomorrow," I said.

"Yes, I am sort of in a daze," Leona answered back. "Thank you for finding me. You don't know how much it meant to me to talk to your mother."

"You are quite welcome. We look forward to talking more and getting to know you. Have a great evening and we'll talk soon."

"Goodbye."

As I hung up the phone my mother said, "Oh my gosh, I don't know what to say. This is just incredible."

I just smiled and said, "Yes, it is. I think it is time to eat. We'll listen to the rest of the tape after supper. Leona shared a lot more about her past and family."

I shouted out to the sunroom, "Dad, it's time to eat."

He laughed and hollered back, "It's about time."

Chapter 24

Leona Hendrickson was born to Clark and Anna Hendrickson on December 29, 1907. She was their third child and second daughter. Her older sister Iva was beautiful and everyone said "she should be one of them Hollywood movie stars." Louis was two years older and Leona absolutely worshiped her brother. He was always there for her when she needed him. Leona's little sister, Goldie, was five years younger. Goldie looked up to Leona and followed her like a puppy. Then there was little Dale, or Bud, her youngest brother. He was a typical pain for a little brother but she wouldn't trade him for the world.

Leona was a self-described tomboy through and through. She loved the outdoors! She started hunting and fishing with her papa when she was very little and would rather be outdoors anytime, even feeding the chickens or gathering eggs, instead of doing chores in the house. Her mama said Leona was a better farmhand than most boys. She could milk the cow faster than even Louis and she had a way with animals. She loved her brown bay pony and rode him all over the pasture with Goldie holding on tight around her waist.

She was Papa's girl, and he left an awful void when he died in 1920 after contracting a terrible fever. Many neighbors lost family members as well. Leona was only 12 years old at the time. After Papa died, the family all worked hard trying to keep the farm going. Louis worked so hard—really hard—trying to replace Papa, but they still could not make ends meet.

The only way to keep the farm was for Leona's mama to marry that Mr. Barton, a man who had been trying to woo Mama ever since the day Papa died. He was so nice and brought her flowers and brought the kids Baby Ruth candy bars. Their lives took a drastic turn the day Mama said she'd marry old man Barton, as the kids called him behind his back. Poor Mama had no idea the old coot drank hooch and was so wretched and mean when he was drunk. Leona often thought, "How could Mama marry that horrible man who could never replace Papa?"

Old man Barton worked the kids to the bone and treated Louis horribly. Leona was so sad the day Louis ran off to find work and get away from Barton. The thought of leaving Mama, Goldie, and Bud alone with that man was heartbreaking, but she knew she too would take off as soon as she could. At the time, she just didn't know how or when.

Chapter 25

♡♡

The Dance, May 10, 1924

Leona and Goldie were nervously walking down the country road. It was a gorgeous spring Saturday evening with the cottonwood trees spreading their silky white seeds everywhere. The first quarter moon was shining brightly and lighting their way. Leona was 16 and Goldie was 12. They were very happy school was out, but they had so much work to do this summer on the farm. Leona, Goldie, and Bud attended the school in Havana. Next year would be Leona's last year of school and then she could leave home and get away from that awful Mr. Barton who had ruined her family.

The Hendrickson girls were dressed in their best dresses as they almost skipped down the dusty road toward Havana. They kept looking over their shoulders to make sure there wasn't anyone behind them. They whispered and giggled together. Leona and Goldie had snuck out of the house to go to the dance for the students who had graduated that year. They knew they could be getting themselves into big trouble, but they didn't care. It was worth the risk.

When they asked Mama a couple days earlier if they could go to the end of the year school dance, old man Barton had grumbled, "NO, you girls ain't goin' nowhere! You got work to do and don't have time to be out gallivanting."

After old man Barton bellowed, "NO!" Mama just gave Leona that tired, sad smile. She knew Mama would have said, "Yes, they could go," but Mama couldn't argue with her new husband. It had happened in the past and Leona was pretty sure old man Barton had slapped his wife across the face and threatened her if she ever talked back to him again. Leona had not seen him hit her mama, but she had seen red marks on her cheeks.

Leona had wanted to say they could stay at Grams and Gramps in Havana, but she knew better than to mention her papa's family in front of old man Barton. All the Hendricksons were well respected in these parts. Leona knew Barton was jealous of all the Hendrickson family but only pretended to like them when they were around.

Gramps was actually not Leona's real grandpa. Her grandpa Amariah Hendrickson died in 1906. Grams married Gramps and moved to town in Havana. Grams' daughter and her husband took over Grandpa Hendrickson's farm, and Leona's parents bought a small farm close to the home place. Leona never knew her real grandpa, but Gramps was a wonderful man and always loved Grams' kids and grandkids as if they were his own. Leona always thought, "Why couldn't Mama have found someone like Gramps to marry instead of old man Barton?"

The girls were so sad and defeated. They moped for two days. On Leona's last day of school, the day before the dance, the other girls in her class asked if she was coming. She said her stepfather wouldn't let her go. They comforted her and chimed in how mean that old goat was. All the girls loved Leona and wanted her to be with them to celebrate at the dance. She also knew Louis, her big brother, would be there and she desperately wanted to see him. Right then and there, Leona's stubbornness set in and she decided she was going to sneak out and go to that dance.

The morning of the dance, before Leona and Goldie got out of their bed, Leona told Goldie her plan. She formulated it before she went to sleep the night before. Leona seriously considered going alone because she didn't want Goldie to get in trouble if they got caught. However, Leona knew if she snuck out and her little sister woke up in the middle of the night, Goldie would get worried and go tell Mama. Leona was also afraid to make the trip by herself, so she asked Goldie if she wanted to go. Goldie was all in. She had to promise not to tell Bud because he couldn't keep a secret, and they couldn't risk getting caught because they would have hell to pay.

Leona hid their dresses in the rafters of the outhouse that morning. After they kissed Mama good night and went to bed, they waited and checked to make sure everyone else was asleep. Old man Barton was snoring two doors down. The girls quietly crawled out of bed and slid across the floor on their bottoms so the creaky floor didn't give them away. Wearing their bed clothes, they made their break to the window.

Leona was first. Ever so gently she lowered herself down to the ground by holding on to the windowsill. Then she helped Goldie down. They stole across the yard to the outhouse, looking back frequently for any movement in the house. They'd thought of everything...except their dogs. Just as they got to the outhouse, the dogs barked and ran toward them. The girls shushed and soothed them. After a few minutes of reassuringly petting them, the contented dogs headed back under the porch to go to sleep.

The girls grabbed their dresses from the rafters, which were exactly where Leona hid them earlier in the day. She knew if they tried to change clothes in the house, odds were old man Barton or Mama would have heard them. Leona had picked out her best hand-me-down dress from her sister, Iva, and Goldie had chosen her blue dress that had been Leona's. Ever since Papa had died, neither one had new dresses of their own. They changed quickly and tucked their bedclothes in the rafters and headed to the dance.

Chapter 26

The moonlight guided them down the gravel road. They were excited to see their school friends but even more excited to see Louis. He just had to be there. They seldom saw him since he had moved away from home to get away from old man Barton. He worked for a rancher close to Sedan, Kansas, for room and board and just a few dollars a month. He wasn't welcome on their farm as old man Barton told Louis he didn't ever want him setting foot on "his" farm again. That just boiled Leona's hide. How dare that sap call it "his" farm and ban Louis. She knew how sad that made Mama.

The girls walked faster as they got closer to town. They could hear the music at the town community building where all the dances were held. Leona recognized the song the band was playing. It was "Oh Johnny, Oh Johnny! Oh!" her favorite song. She loved dancing to it.

As she and Goldie reached the open door, she immediately scanned the room for her Louis. He spotted them first and began waving his arms to get their attention. They ran across the room to him. He scooped Goldie up in his arms and swung her around a couple times. He sat her down and put both arms around Leona and gave her a big hug. "I've missed you two so much. How're my girls?"

"We're really happy NOW seeing you," Leona said hugging Louis harder.

"How the heck did you get Barton to let you come to the dance?" Louis asked.

Leona had a smirk and Goldie looked down. Louis knew right away they snuck out. Leona said defiantly, "We wanted to come, so we did. We asked Mama and old man Barton said absolutely not. So we hid our clothes in the outhouse and snuck out."

"You little devils. You better not get caught going back or you sure will get your hides tanned. But I'm awful happy you're here."

After the short reunion, Goldie pulled Louis out to the dance floor while Leona headed over to her girlfriends to chat. They were commenting on each other's dresses, school being out and what they were going to do over the summer when a smartly dressed, handsome boy with dark brown hair strolled by. Leona thought he was the most handsome boy she had ever seen. He could have been a movie star. She whispered to her friend Vena Mae, "Who is that?"

Vena Mae giggled and said, "Why Ona, that's Nick Belt. All his friends call him Burgie. He lives on a farm over by Hale."

Hale was even a smaller town than Havana. Hale was about 10 miles northwest of Havana as the crow flies, but the road zigzagged back and forth and was about 15 miles. "Nick's father is a big-time farmer over there and has lots of land and money. His dad is one of the first men in these parts to own an automobile. Nick even gets to drive it some people say."

Leona couldn't pull her eyes off Nick until he turned and looked her way. Her eyes darted down to the floor but it was too late. Nick had already seen that she had been looking at him. "Oh no," she said after glancing back up, "he's coming toward us."

She had never been timid, but all of a sudden she was all butterflies and felt like she should run. Her legs wouldn't move though and before she knew it, Nick was standing right in front of her.

Nick reached out his hand toward her. "Hello. My name's Nick but all my friends call me Burgie," he said confidently. "You should call me Burgie, too."

Leona blushed. She took his hand and shook it. Her body warmed all over and she felt like she would melt. But her bold nature took over and she spoke up saying, "Well, I kind of like the name Nick. Burgie is such a silly name. I think I will call you Nick instead." She smiled and looked him straight into his brown eyes.

"And what's your name?" he asked smiling.

In a defiant, confident tone she answered, "I'm Leona May Hendrickson. All MY friends call me Ona, but YOU can call me Leona."

Nick grinned and said "Well, Leona it is. Would you like to dance, Miss Leona May Hendrickson?"

He didn't give her a chance to answer but pulled her toward the dance floor. She felt giddy and as if she was in a trance. It was like that book she read at school and she was Cinderella and was dancing with Prince Charming. It was magical. She wished it would never end.

To her surprise, Nick continued to dance with her after the first dance. He seemed to be as smitten with her as she was with him. He was a very smooth talker and totally captivated Leona. After several dances, this wonderful evening was coming to a close too rapidly.

Louis caught her eye and motioned for her to come over to where he and Goldie were standing. Leona excused herself telling Nick she needed to go talk to her brother and sister. Nick smiled and said, "Well, you don't be gone too long, Leona Hendrickson."

Louis grinned at his little sister as she came up to them and asked if she was having a good time. Leona blushed and said it was all right, but she was bursting with joy. Louis told the girls it was getting late and they had better hurry back home before Mama and that evil man noticed they were gone. Leona said, "Yes, you are right. We should be getting back. Just a second, I'll be right back."

Goldie and Louis watched as Leona ran to Nick and told him she needed to get home. He looked disappointed, saying "But it's still so early."

Leona apologized but said it was time for her to leave. It was getting late and she needed to get her little sister home. Nick took her hand and thanked her for dancing and the wonderful night. He asked, "When can I see you again?"

Her heart fluttered. He wanted to see her again! She knew her mean stepfather would never let her date anyone so she paused. "Well, there is a dance here next week. Maybe we could meet then?" she asked.

Nick smiled and said he would be there with bells on. She smiled bashfully and pulled her hand back. She ran across the room and hugged Louis. She took Goldie's hand and they ran to the door as she waved to her friends. She stole one last look at Nick and he gave his toothy, sly grin and winked.

The girls practically ran all the way home without hardly saying a word. Leona was thinking of her quick exit from her "Prince Charming" and thought of Cinderella and how she lost her glass slipper rushing to get home before midnight. She smiled and looked down at the shoes on her feet.

They slowed as they got closer and caught their breaths. Quietly on tiptoes, they snuck across the apple orchard then through the backyard to the outhouse and their bedclothes' hiding place. They quickly changed without uttering a peep. The girls reached the bedroom window without stirring the sleeping dogs and climbed back into their room.

Leona and Goldie scooted across the old wooden floor and slid back into bed. Safely under the covers, the two girls whispered, reliving the night at the dance and Goldie quickly fell asleep. Leona was wide awake, thoughts about Nick swimming in her head. He really seemed to like her—yes, her—Leona Hendrickson. She had danced with the most handsome boy at the dance.

Chapter 27

The next week was torture for the girls and Bud. Old man Barton lined up job after job for them to do. Cleaning the chicken coop, scooping out the barn stalls, weeding the garden, spring cleaning the house from top to bottom, and washing all the bedding and clothes. He also decided it was time to butcher the fat hog. They had several neighbors who came over to help with the process.

The hog was killed and hung to drain the blood. Then the carcass was scalded with boiling water to help remove the hair. Once gutted and cleaned, it was cut up into pieces and some of the meat was cured by smoking. The men took care of the smoking and the rest of the meat was canned by the women, using glass Mason jars for containers.

The fat that had been removed had to be rendered. It needed to be cut into smaller cubes, which was Leona and Goldie's job. Goldie thought it was gross but Leona, always the tomboy, thought nothing of the greasy work. The fat cubes were placed in a big black kettle where the fat was slowly heated and began to liquefy. The girls had to constantly keep stirring the fat to keep it from sticking and burning.

Once the fat was melted completely, a couple of the men would lift the heavy kettle and pour some of the liquid into the lard press. Most of the liquid fat ran through the press and into a bucket. Then it took both Leona's and Goldie's strength together to turn the press to squeeze the remaining lard out and into the bucket.

After cranking the press and squeezing out all of the liquid lard, all that remained were the cracklings. These remaining cooked bits were salted and tasted delicious as the girls snacked on them throughout the rest of the day.

At the end of the week, the girls helped Mama and the men who helped with the butchering make panhas, which is what Papa had always called it. Old man Barton called it scrapple but what did he know.

Panhas is kind of a mush that includes the leftover pork scraps that couldn't be used or sold, such as the head, heart, liver, and other trimmings. These were all boiled to make a broth and again it was the girls' job to help stir this constantly while it was cooking in the big, black kettle over the fire. They used a big wooden ladle to keep the boiling meat stirred.

Once the cooked bones and layer of liquid fat floating at the top were discarded, the meat was scooped out and set to the side. Bud's job was to keep the flies off the meat and he swiped his hand in a steady rhythm to scare off the flies.

Next, the leftover broth had cornmeal and flour slowly added to make a mush. Leona barely could stir the thickened broth as it got thicker and thicker. One of the men took the giant wooden ladle from Leona and continued to stir the mush.

The meat was minced into very small pieces and added to the mush along with salt and spices sage, thyme, and black pepper. It was now so hard to stir that the thick conglomeration required three men to take turns stirring the mush.

After the panhas was completely mixed together, they poured it into pans or formed into loaves and set aside to cool. All the workers would take some home to their families to enjoy.

Old man Barton always wanted his "scrapple" for breakfast. Mama would cut thin half-inch slices and pan fry the panhas until it was brown and had a nice crust. The Hendricksons always put butter on *their* panhas, then maple syrup. But old man Barton was such a saphead. He wanted scrambled eggs with his scrapple and would cover them both with Mama's homemade ketchup and horseradish. No wonder the old coot was so mean.

Chapter 28

May 17, 1924

As the week slowly went by, Leona could not get her mind off of Nick. He was such a gentleman and treated her like she was a princess at the dance. She was going to have to sneak out again, but she didn't want Goldie to go with her this time.

Come Saturday morning without Goldie knowing, Leona slipped her dress again in the hiding place. She was in a very good mood all day and even old man Barton's yelling at her for not watering the garden first thing in the morning couldn't ruin Leona's day.

That night she and Goldie went to bed. She knew Goldie was exhausted from all the work they had done that day and would fall asleep quickly. She waited until she knew Goldie was out. She slipped out of bed and slid across the floor to keep it from creaking and waking Goldie or anyone else in the house. The window was already open as it was a beautiful spring night. Leona slid out the window and as quietly as an elk hunter in tall grass, she crept to the outhouse where she retrieved her clothes and changed quickly and quietly.

The moon was full and the added brightness was reassuring to Leona since she was making the trip alone without Goldie by her side. Leona could hardly remember the trip. Her feet carried her as quickly as they could. Tonight's dance was a town dance held in Havana every two weeks. She ran up to the same familiar town community building where the school dance had been held. She opened the door to hear laughter and music. This time the room was filled with smoke. No smoking had been allowed at the school graduation dance. It reminded her of when old man Barton was smoking on the back porch and made her wince.

Glancing around the room, Leona quickly spotted her girlfriends and waved. She ran to them and they all asked what had taken her so long to get there. She continued to look around the room and there was Louis out dancing with her friend, Mabel. They were cutting a rug and really having a good time. Louis didn't see her as he was too focused on Mabel.

Just then she saw him. Nick was talking to a couple other guys and must have been telling some good stories as they were laughing and slapping each other on their backs. She waited and chatted with her friends but never took an eye off of Nick. Finally Nick turned and saw her. The smile on his face lit up the entire place. He headed to her. Leona swooned with excitement.

"Hello, beautiful," he whispered in her ear.

She blushed and smiled back at him. He led her to the dance floor and she floated in Nick's arms. They danced and danced. Nick leaned in and asked if she needed something to drink and some fresh air. She said, "Absolutely."

Nick grabbed some cups of water and handed one to Leona and guided her outside to where the fresh night air immediately cooled the sweaty dancers. They talked and Nick asked about her family. He said he had met Louis at the ranch where he worked. Nick and his brother had gone over to help them work the spring calves. He said Louis seemed like a nice guy and a real hard worker. Leona beamed with pride to hear Nick brag about her big brother.

He asked about the rest of her family and she told Nick about Mama and about her sisters, Iva and Goldie, and other brother, Bud. Leona shared about losing her papa, and even about mean old man Barton. While she talked about her papa, tears filled her eyes. Nick wiped the tear that rolled down her cheek and told her he was so sorry.

Leona looked into Nick's brown eyes and she had never had this feeling before. She wondered, "Is this what it feels like to fall in love?"

Nick's eyes sparkled in the moonlight, and he leaned in and kissed her. This was Leona's very first real kiss. She didn't count her classmate Clem's little peck behind the school building last fall. Leona had never felt so loved and appreciated since her papa died. Nick and Leona's kiss lingered. When the kiss finally broke, Leona could see Nick's brown eyes sparkling at her in the moonlight. He said, "Let's go for a walk." She wanted nothing more than to spend more time alone with this handsome man that made her feel loved.

Chapter 29

Leona was so glad the moon was full and bright as it guided her way home. If anything, it was even brighter than when she left the farm to go to the dance. Maybe it was just because her mind was so filled with happy thoughts. Everything seemed better.

It was later than she had planned to get home. She didn't even go back to the dance to say goodbye to Louis. After spending time with Nick alone, she knew she needed to get home and didn't want to go back to the dance anyway. Nick walked her to the edge of town on her way home before kissing her goodbye.

Arriving home, she began her foolproof ritual. She crept across the yard to the outhouse and changed her clothes. Even if she didn't get caught sneaking in, the smoke that permeated her clothes and hair would be a dead giveaway. She made her way to the old pump and quietly pumped water into the basin and used some homemade lye soap left for the farmhands to wash up. The lye definitely helped cut the smoke smell.

Leona climbed in through the bedroom window. She was worried about the smoky smell in her hair. She went to her dresser, picked up her hair brush, and diligently brushed her hair. She quietly crawled into bed and pulled the covers up over her. She made it back into bed without waking Goldie! Her mind raced as she thought back over the evening and oh, that first kiss. She was filled with such mixed emotions. She felt excited, guilty, loved, ashamed, special and alone all at the same time. How could that be? What happened? Did Nick really love her like he had said? How did she ever let him do to her what he did? Was it wrong when you love someone like she loved Nick? No one had loved her the way he did. The way he held her and looked in her eyes and made her feel special and like she was the only girl alive. After Nick made love to her, he held her and told her he loved her and wanted to marry her. She smiled and told him she loved him too. They would be together forever. She would leave old man Barton's roof and never come back again. Leona drifted to sleep with a faint smile on her face.

Chapter 30

The idea of marrying Nick and getting way from old man Barton was all Leona could think of during the next few days. She was so happy. Mama noticed something was different about her. While they were washing clothes that late spring afternoon, Mama turned to Leona and asked, "Leona, are you okay? You seem to be very distracted."

"I'm fine, Mama," she answered fibbing. "I've just been thinking about Louis and what he's doing. We used to talk about things we want to do and places we want to go."

"Well, young'n, right now you need to be thinking about the work you have to do and all that other stuff will come when it comes."

"Yes, Mama," Leona replied.

The week drug along slowly but Leona couldn't get her mind off Nick. She wanted to see him so badly, but she didn't know how she could get to see him. The next dance wasn't for another whole week. She knew Mama wouldn't let her take off to go look for no boy.

May 31, 1924

Two agonizing weeks passed since Leona saw Nick. It was time to sneak out again and go see him at the dance. She followed the same plan and Goldie fell asleep early. It didn't take long and Leona was heading to the dance. It was almost a new moon and there wasn't much light to guide her. It was a little spooky without the bright moonlight as in previous trips. It forced her to walk slowly and cautiously, avoiding rocks and potholes. She made it to town and the community building once again. She could hear the music, laughter and loud voices.

As Leona entered the noisy room, her eyes roamed the room. No Nick. She spotted Louis in his green shirt, suspenders, and new cowboy hat. He looked very handsome and she knew all the girls were interested in him. He waved his hat at her. She ran to him and gave him a hug. It had been way too long since she had seen her big brother. "You have a good time at the last dance, Ona? I didn't see you leave and was kinda worried if you was okay."

"Oh yes, I had a great time. I was fine. You was dancing and I just needed to get on home and didn't want to bother you," Leona fibbed and looked around the room.

Louis could tell something was on her mind. "Ona, what's going on?" he asked.

"Nothing, Louis, just looking for someone," as she continued to scan the room.

"Who you looking for, Sis?"

"Nick Belt. I was dancing with him the last time I was here."

"You mooning over Nick Belt, Ona?" Louis asked.

Leona gave her brother a disgusted look but she couldn't hide that she liked Nick.

"I haven't seen him tonight. He might have gone over to Sedan. They're having a dance there tonight too. I saw him over there last weekend. They have a dance there every week," Louis told her.

Leona's heart sank. Nick was not here. He surely knew she would be here tonight. She promised she would come tonight and he said he would too. She stayed close to Louis most of the night when he wasn't out dancing. She barely talked to her friends and when she did, they kept asking what was wrong. She lied, saying she was just tired from all the work on the farm. Thankfully whenever the band was playing, her friends would go off dancing and leave her alone to sit in the corner.

She searched the room again and again. There was no sign of Nick. She kept her eyes on the door. Still no Nick. She was extremely anxious and was unable to have a good time. When one of Louis' friends finally asked Leona to dance, she told the young man she was too tired. She really just didn't want to dance with anyone but Nick.

It was getting late and it was obvious that Nick was not coming. She had to get home and get to bed before she was caught. She gave Louis a big hug and told him she would look for him at the next dance in two weeks if he would be there. Louis asked, "If I see Nick, is there anything you want me to say to him?"

Leona thought about it and said, "Yes, just tell him I'll be here in two weeks at the dance and hope to see him. Thank you, Louis. You're a wonderful big brother."

It was a very long walk home in the dark.

Chapter 31

June 14, 1924

The next two weeks were painfully long for Leona. As the days got longer, there was more work to be done on the farm. It rained for two solid days and that meant less time working in the garden and outdoors, more time trapped in the house. In the evening after chores were done, Leona loved going down to the pond fishing, but the ponds were too full and the fishing wasn't good. How she loved hunting and fishing with Louis. He teased her that she was all tomboy and could out shoot any boy in Montgomery and Chautauqua Counties.

The wheat was turning a light gold. Once it was ready to harvest, the next few weeks would be torturous. It was exhausting work for the men and boys harvesting, the women cooking meals over the hot stoves in the summer heat to keep the menfolk fed, and the girls and youngest boys hauling water for the men and horses in the fields.

The only way to be able to complete the harvest before Mother Nature destroyed the wheat was for all neighbors to work together—cutting the wheat, binding into shocks, gathering the dried shocks, and threshing the wheat to separate the wheat kernels from the stalks.

During harvest, there would be no dances in town. The next dance wouldn't be until fair time, toward the end of July. This Saturday's dance before harvest was her last chance to see Nick for some time.

The morning of the dance, Goldie and Leona fed the chickens and gathered the morning eggs in the chicken coop. Goldie quickly jerked her hand back as an old mean hen pecked at her while she tried to get the hen's precious egg. Leona laughed and said, "When are you going to learn that you can't just stick your hand under that old hen without getting pecked? You have to put your arm up against her and slide under."

"I know, I know," Goldie rolled her eyes at her big sis who was making fun of her. She took Leona's advice and retrieved, uninjured, the beautiful, brown egg. She turned to Leona and said, "I know tonight is the dance in town, and I want to go with you again this time."

Leona looked at her and replied, "I'm not going to the dance. You know Mama will never let us go. Besides, I'm just too tired after all this work we have to do."

"Well, it didn't stop you the last two times."

Leona was stunned. Did Goldie really know she'd gone to the dances? Leona probed, "What do you mean?"

"I know you done snuck out and gone to them dances by yourself," she retorted with an ornery grin on her face. "I've woke up and you were gone so I figured you'd snuck out and went to the dance. I want to go again this time and see Louis."

Knowing she was caught and her plan was dead in the water she said, "Sis, I don't think that's a good idea. If old man Barton finds out, you'll get in so much trouble. It was too risky last time you went."

"I don't care. I want to see Louis and you can't keep me from going or I'll tell Mama you have gone the last two times."

Leona was trapped. She scowled at Goldie but had no choice but to let her little sister go with her again if she was going to get to see Nick. She knew Goldie missed Louis as much as she did. "Okay, you have to promise me though that you'll stay with Louis and not wander off," she grumbled. "I have to find you when it's time to come home."

"I promise, Ona. Thank you. I miss Louis so much."

Actually, Leona was really happy to have the company going to town, but she really didn't want Goldie tagging along with her when she got to see Nick. If Nick wanted to go for a walk again, she had to make sure Goldie stayed with Louis. Louis better be there tonight is all she could think.

The girls hid their dresses in their outhouse right after they finished their lunch and old man Barton was taking his nap to let his food digest.

Chapter 32

That evening the girls again initiated their escape and slipped out the window. They had to be extra careful tonight as they made their way to the outhouse because farmhands slept in the loft of the barn during harvest. They sure didn't want to come across one of them sitting in the outhouse.

They changed out of their bedclothes and put on their party dresses and shoes. Leona motioned to Goldie with a finger over her lips not to say anything. It was close to another full moon so they had pretty good light to walk from shadow to shadow of the trees in the apple orchard until they got to the road. Arm-in-arm the girls walked quickly down the road toward their destination. Leona would never tell Goldie but she was secretly comforted having her little sister with her. She was worried. What if Nick wasn't at the dance? She would be happy to have Goldie with her coming home.

The sisters clipped right along the well-lit road. They heard the familiar music at the community building. They saw several people standing outside. There were horses and buggies and also a couple of those horseless buggies parked along the street. Leona and Goldie were yet to ride in an automobile. Old man Barton said they were the devil's work and, though he probably could afford one, wouldn't think of paying money for something the devil himself had created. Nick told Leona that his father had an automobile made by Henry Ford and he had even driven it. Leona dreamed of the day when Nick took her for a ride and she would wave at all her friends as they went down Main Street of Havana.

The girls made their way into the dance. It was hot and humid and the cigarette smoke in the air was thick and heavy. It was much more crowded than it had been the other nights. She was sure everyone knew it was going to be their last chance to get together and dance before harvest and everyone was ready to cut loose. She and Goldie saw several friends and stopped and chatted.

They looked and looked but couldn't find Louis. All of a sudden Goldie shrieked and broke free from Leona's arm. Leona saw Louis almost at the same time and a huge smile was on his face. He lifted Goldie up as she leaped into his arms and gave each other a big hug. "Baby girl, I think you have grown five inches since last time I saw you," Louis teased.

Leona went to Louis and gave him a big hug. As always, he looked really tall and handsome. He winked at Leona and asked what she was doing babysitting this little kid. Goldie smacked him hard in his stomach and he doubled over pretending to be in terrible pain. They all laughed. It was so great to be together again. Louis told Goldie her best friend, Mildred, was over by the south window. She gave him another hug and said she would be right back. She skipped across the now quiet dance floor as the band was taking a little break.

Louis looked at Leona knowing the question behind those inquisitive eyes. "How are you, Sis? How is Mama and Bud?"

Leona answered as expected. "They are doing the best they can under the circumstances. Bud never complains and just does his work. Mama never smiles, and old man Barton is as mean as ever."

It just about made Louis blow his top and he wanted to beat that old man to a pulp. Leona never told Louis about her fear that Barton hit Mama because she knew Louis probably would kill him.

Louis looked her in the eyes and said, "I haven't seen Nick here tonight, Ona. He was at the dance in Sedan again last week." A look of question came across her face. She wanted to know if he had talked to him.

"I told him what you had said," he hesitated. Leona looked at him and begged to hear more. "He told me that you were a sweet gal and he really liked you a lot but his dad was keeping him pretty busy, and he didn't know when he would be back over this way. Ona, he is a rounder. He had gals hanging all over him at the dance in Sedan. Honey, he's trouble. You just need to forget him."

Tears welled up in her eyes and Louis knew these words broke her heart. He hated seeing his little sister so upset. He always wanted to protect her from getting hurt. He put his arms around her and pulled her into him. His hug always comforted Leona, but she knew this feeling was not going to go away with a hug. He said to her, "Sweetie, there are a lot guys out there that will treat you much better. You just wait and see. The right guy will come along."

All Leona could think about was Nick and how he had told her he loved her. She was sick to her stomach now and just wanted to go home. She asked Louis if he could go get Goldie because she wanted to go home.

Goldie wasn't ready to go when Louis found her. "Leona isn't feeling good so you need to head home," he said.

She frowned saying, "But we just got here. I don't want to go yet."

"I know, Sis. I think Leona is just worn out from working so hard, and the heat and smoke are getting to her," he fibbed. "Go spend a little time with your friends and tell them goodbye. I'll walk you home. Leona and I'll wait for you outside in the cooler air. Don't be too long."

Goldie went and told her friends goodbye. She found her siblings outside and took Louis' arm to start home. At least she would get to spend time with Louis.

Chapter 33

It was a beautiful moonlit night with just a few clouds floating by to block the moon every now and then. It was so good to have Louis there with them as the three made their way down the gravel road, kicking stones. They walked side-by-side with one of Louis' arms around each girl. Leona felt some comfort having Louis with her after the disappointment about Nick. They decided to go a block out of their way and walk by their grandparents' house. How they wished they were awake so they could stop and say "hi."

Louis stayed with Grams and Gramps when he first moved off Papa and Mama's farm. He told the girls that they were getting kind of feeble and should ask Mama if they could take Bud and go visit them. Leona liked that idea and would ask Mama sometime when Barton wasn't around. Mama always loved Grams and Gramps but didn't get to see them much since Papa had died.

Leona knew Mama could send them to town on an errand so they could see Grams and Gramps without old man Barton knowing. They walked toward the farm and chatted and Louis and Goldie teased one another. This banter made Leona smile and helped ease the devastation of not seeing Nick.

Reaching the edge of the apple orchard, Louis said, "This is as far as I better go. Goodbye, squirt," as he gave Goldie a hug.

When he hugged Leona, he whispered in her ear, "Ona, it is going to be okay. Just forget about Nick."

Leona and Goldie quietly crossed the orchard to the outhouse and again changed clothes. They washed up and snuck back to the house. They went through the window and got into bed. They were exhausted. As usual, it took Goldie mere seconds to fall asleep but Leona was wide awake. "Why hadn't Nick been there?" She kept thinking about what Louis said about Nick being a rounder. Her mind was spinning. "He said he loved me. Maybe he couldn't get to town for the dance. If I could just see him and talk to him. Can I ever forget him like Louis said?"

Chapter 34

June 18, 1924

Leona, Goldie, and Bud were busy with chores from sunrise to sunset. One morning Leona and Mama washed clothes and it was just the two of them hanging the wet clothes on the line. "Mama, could the kids and I go and visit Grams and Gramps? It's been so long since we got to see them. Once harvest starts next week, we won't ever get to see them."

Mama said, "Honey, I know how much you miss seeing them. Grams' birthday is coming up and I want to send some canned goods and a pecan pie to her so how about you kids take them to her for me on Saturday?"

Leona was ecstatic. She grabbed her mama and kissed her on her cheek. This was Wednesday so in just three days they would be able to get off the farm. "Can I go tell Goldie and Bud?"

"Sure, I'll finish hanging up these clothes but hurry right back so you can help me start fixin' lunch." Leona headed off to look for her brother and sister to give them the good news.

Recently Leona hadn't felt too good and had an upset stomach, mostly in the morning. When Mama noticed that Leona's appetite seemed to be next to nothing, she asked her daughter if she felt okay. Leona said she was just tired and her stomach had been bothering her but probably because she ate too many tomatoes right out of the garden. She seemed to feel better once the day wore on.

Finally Saturday arrived and Mama put canned goods and Grams' favorite pecan pie into the wicker basket for the kids to carry. She also put a hand-crocheted doily in the basket for Grams' birthday. Mr. Barton was not happy when she told him the kids were going to go to town on Saturday when there was work to be done. He begrudgingly agreed and the fact it rained Friday night helped matters. Mama gave Leona the basket and told the two younger children to behave and listen to Leona. Bud said, "Yes, ma'am," as he knew she was directing the order to him.

The three Hendrickson children headed for town though it was a little tricky with the muddy road. They decided to walk in the pasture beside the road instead. The three took turns carrying the heavy basket of goodies though Leona did most of the time. As they approached town, Bud asked Leona if Louis would be there. She didn't know but sure hoped he would be.

They got to their grandparents' house and walked right in without knocking. Grams ran to each of them and gave them a huge hug. She said, "My lands, it's my grandbabies. This is the best birthday present ever."

Leona handed Grams the basket of goodies. The kids could tell from the smell coming from the kitchen that Grams had been baking all morning. She steered the kids to the kitchen and put the basket on the kitchen table. Just as Grams started to open the basket, Gramps and Louis came in from the parlor.

"Well, I declare, look what the cat drug in," Gramps teased. Bud ran to him and flung his arms around his waist while Gramps gave his grandson an affectionate pat on the head. The girls went to Gramps and got their hugs while Louis put Bud in an arm hold and gave him a good "Dutch rub" on the top of the head that made Bud squeal. Louis gave each girl a hug and threatened to give them a "Dutch rub."

Grams shooed the menfolk out of her kitchen and enlisted the girls' help to get lunch on the table. She put out quite a spread of fried chicken, potato salad, bread-and-butter pickles, canned beets, and radishes right from the garden. When they called the men to the table, Gramps said "grace" and they all dug in eating. Bud went right for a drumstick. Goldie loved Grams' potato salad. Louis stacked his plate high with a little of everything. Grams had an eye on Leona and said, "Ona, what happened to your appetite? You are barely touching your food."

"I don't know Grams. It all looks wonderful. I guess I don't know where to start. I haven't been very hungry lately. My stomach's been a little queasy. Must be all this summer heat."

"Well, if you don't get to eaten' and feeling better, I'm getting some castor oil down you and that will cure what ails you."

With that idea, Leona decided she better try and eat something for the thought of castor oil was way worse than any upset stomach. After a few bites of Grams' potato salad she actually felt a little better. The rest of the meal was filled with laughter and remembering all the great times they had in years past. The kids asked Grams to tell them some more stories about their papa when he was a kid. She had some great ones. Lunch went by way too fast. Grams said, "I am going to cut your mama's pecan pie for dessert. Anybody want some?"

Bud almost came up out of his chair in excitement at the idea. "You bet! I love Mama's pecan pie."

After lunch was over and the dishes were done, Louis needed to get back to the Robish ranch and check on the cattle and make sure none of them got spooked the night before from the thunderstorm. Leona, Goldie and Bud gathered up their empty basket and told Grams and Gramps they needed to head back to the farm. Grams said, "You ain't leaving with no empty basket."

Grams went to her pie cabinet where she had some tomato preserves and wild plum jelly. She got a jar of each and put them in the basket. "Now you be careful going home and don't drop this basket. You give your mama a hug for me and thank her for the beautiful doily. Your mama has always been the best crocheter in the family," she said. "Now don't be strangers. Come back and visit Gramps and me real soon."

One final hug and the three Hendrickson children started on their way home. The road was pretty dry now so they didn't have to walk out in the pasture and it would be much faster going, not that they were in any hurry to get home. That old man Barton would just put them to work the minute they stepped on the place. They wondered if they would have hell to pay for being gone all day.

Chapter 35

Summer flew by. Harvest was over but there was always work to be done on the farm. Leona never made it back to town for a dance. Her heart ached for Nick. Did he miss her the way she missed him? Was he afraid of old man Barton and that's what kept him away? She dreamed of Nick showing up in his car some day and taking her away from all of this. He loved her. He told her so. Her sweet daydreams were being frequently interrupted by a piercing thought. What if he lied? What if he didn't love her? What if he was seeing another girl? She pushed those thoughts aside. At least she was finally feeling a little better, still tired but her queasiness was gone.

School would be starting soon after Labor Day. She was so ready to be able to get back to her studies and spend time with her girlfriends. They were going to have a new teacher this year as Miss Darting got married and moved to Cedar Vale. Their new teacher was going to be Mr. Hedges from Independence. Leona thought it would be fun to have a man as teacher for a change. Surely he couldn't be as strict as Miss Darting.

After the first day of school, Leona discovered how wrong she had been about Mr. Hedges. He never smiled once the whole first day of school. He lined out all the expectations for each grade and how older students would help younger students and who was paired with whom. Goldie was sitting about half way back while Leona was on the back row. Bud was right up front. Leona was sure it was because Bud was one of the younger ones but also because Mr. Hedges knew he needed to keep an eye on him.

Leona's favorite subject was math. She was pretty good at it and almost always won any math contests. Now spelling was another thing. She was always the first one out in the school spelling bees. It was a joke amongst the girls that Ona couldn't spell her way out of a gunnysack.

One fall day at lunch, Leona and her friend Edna were sitting out in the schoolyard under a big cottonwood tree. Edna had a beat-up metal lunch pail, but Leona just had a flour sack to carry her lunch. Both girls had some homemade bread. Leona had apple butter her mama made from this season's Jonathan apples from the orchard. Out of the blue Edna said, "Ona, you look like your bosom's getting bigger than mine. Looks like you need a bigger camisole."

Leona glanced down comparing the two girls' chests.

"I'm getting jealous," Edna teased. "Maybe your mama's apple butter is doing that to you and you need to share some with me," Edna laughed.

Leona scoffed at her friend, but she had noticed how her bosom was filling out and was a little sensitive. Her tummy was not as flat as it had been. Mama was always skin and bones, but Grams was a pretty, plump, big bosomed woman. She wondered if she was going to be built like Grams. She sure hoped not, but Leona was going to have to start wearing one of her sister Iva's larger hand-me-down camisoles.

It was a just a couple days later that a frightened Goldie came running to Leona. Goldie was white as a ghost. "Goldie, what's the matter?" Leona asked.

Goldie was terrified. Leona could hardly hear her little sister mutter a few words. She put her arms around Goldie and told her, "It's okay, Sis. Just tell me, what's the matter?"

Through sobs, Goldie eventually told Leona she was dying. She had some blood in her bloomers that morning and just knew she was going to die. Leona broke into a big smile, put her hand on Goldie's head holding her close to her chest so she couldn't look up and see her grinning. Leona struggled to keep from laughing out loud and not make her little sister feel even worse. She kept hugging and rocking Goldie while she comforted her. "Now, now you ain't dying, Goldie. That's just you becoming a woman. You're growing up, Sis."

Leona thought back to how scared she had been. Thankfully she was able to talk to her sister Iva when she too thought she was dying. Poor Iva had said during her first time she didn't have anyone to ask, being the oldest sister. One didn't talk to Mama about such things. Leona went on to explain to Goldie about "that time of the month." Goldie was shocked but also so relieved to know she wasn't dying after all. Goldie continued to hug her sister.

It was while Leona was talking to Goldie that it dawned on her. She couldn't remember the last time she had her period. It wasn't uncommon for her to miss a time or two in the summer when they were working so hard but now that they were back in school, she realized it had been almost five months. "Oh, it couldn't be!" a panicked Leona thought to herself. She had put on some weight. She had felt queasy for several weeks. She and Nick had only been together one time. Could you get pregnant the first time? She thought he loved her and told her he did. What would she do if she was? How embarrassed her Mama, Grams, and Gramps would be. She couldn't be pregnant and not married.

Leona was scared to death and she prayed that she would have her period. Weeks went by. In early October, Leona had to steady herself standing next to her desk because she felt something move. Nobody else in the school seemed to feel it. Reality struck. Leona felt the baby move for the first time. She kept telling herself the little weight she was putting on was her getting older and she was going to be built more like Grams. But there was no denying it now. She felt the baby move. It was a living being inside her. Nick's baby. "Dear Lord, what am I going to do?" Later that night in bed, Leona thought back to when she felt the baby move and began to cry. She was so ashamed. She had not told anybody about what she and Nick had done and never planned to.

Chapter 36

Nobody knew what was bothering Leona, but Mama and Goldie were getting worried. Leona was very quiet and kept to herself. Mama noticed Leona seemed different but for the past few weeks life had been hell with her husband. Mr. Barton's drinking was worse and he was getting meaner. She tried to stay out of his way whenever possible and she assumed that was what also was troubling Leona.

Mama was running short of some supplies and suggested that Leona and the kids go to town on Saturday. It would get them off the farm and away from Mr. Barton for the day. The kids did not have to be told twice. They practically ran to get ready.

Grams was so surprised and excited when the kids came walking into the house. She had longed to see them for weeks. She also had a surprise for them. Louis was now working for the Smith family in town at the hardware store and was staying with Gramps and Grams. Louis liked working at the ranch but wasn't making much money. Gramps had been talking to Mr. Smith one day at the store and Mr. Smith mentioned he was needing some help because business was booming. Gramps suggested Louis and Mr. Smith told him to have Louis stop by. Louis got the job and was making twice the money. The news hadn't made it to the farm yet so this was a complete surprise for the Hendrickson children.

Grams told her grandkids, "Louis is working this morning but he will be home for lunch and has the afternoon off to visit with you. It's so wonderful having him here staying with us for a while.

I'd better get to cooking since I have more mouths to feed then I had planned."

Leona was excited that Louis was going to be there for lunch and all afternoon. She had been trying to figure out what she was going to do. She planned on telling Grams first that she was pregnant. She just couldn't bring herself to tell Mama. Mama's life was so horrible with old man Barton she couldn't bear to be making it worse. Leona so missed her big sister, Iva. She could have told Iva anything and knew Iva would still love her as much as always. But now that she knew Louis was going to be there, she knew she could trust him to help her break the news to Grams, if she could get up the nerve to tell her brother.

Grams took one look at Leona and knew the minute she saw her that she was pregnant. She had her suspicions something was wrong at the last visit. Leona wasn't the first pregnant girl she had ever seen, that was for sure. But Grams knew she needed to wait for Leona to come and talk to her. She didn't want to embarrass her granddaughter and knew what pain she must be dealing with in this difficult time. So she waited and went about her business getting lunch ready and chatting up the kids.

Louis made it home for lunch and let out a whoop when he saw the kids there. "How the heck did you know I was staying here?" he asked.

"Oh, they didn't," Grams said. "They came to see me, not you," she joked and poked him in the side. They all laughed and Louis gave them each a hug and of course, the usual Dutch rub.

Grams told Louis he needed to go wash up. She asked Leona to fetch the clean towels out on the line and give one to Louis. Meanwhile, Goldie and Bud were to help her finish getting lunch ready and to set the dining room table.

Leona went and got the towels and found Louis just ready to dry off his face, arms and hands. After he took a towel and was all dry, he looked at Leona and said, "Okay, Ona, what's wrong? I know that look."

Her dark brown hair was curling around her slim face. A tear began to form in the corner of her eye. She covered her face with her hands, turned from Louis and began to sob. Leona was always the tough one of the bunch. For her to be crying, Louis was almost in shock. His first thought was that something must be wrong with Mama.

"Ona, what's the matter? Is Mama okay?" Louis asked with a sinking feeling in his stomach as he gently held her shoulders and turned her toward him.

"Yes, Mama is okay. But oh, Louis, I am so ashamed."

"Sis, what're you talking about? What's happened?" as he took her in his arms.

Leona was sobbing heavily now and could hardly talk. Just having Louis hold her was what she needed. She was a very strong gal but this had just been so much to keep to herself for so long. Finally, Louis pulled her head back and looked into her eyes. "Ona, what's the matter? It's me, you know you can tell me anything."

She looked in his big brown eyes then looked down and whispered, "I'm pregnant."

What? He was at a loss. Louis was in shock. He was glad Leona was looking down because he was sure the look on his face would have just upset her even more. He regained his composure and asked, "Are you sure? Have you talked to Mama or Grams?"

"No, I haven't told anyone, Louis. But I know I am. I have no doubt. Louis, you can't tell anyone."

Louis brushed the hair from his little sister's face. He knew just how bad she was hurting and his heart was crushed. He would do anything to make her feel better. "Ona, this isn't something we can keep to ourselves. You're going to have to tell Mama and I think we need to tell Grams and Gramps."

"Louis, they're going to hate me."

"No, they won't. They love you," he said.

Louis held her tight for a few minutes without saying anything then quietly asked, "Ona, who's the father?"

Leona looked down again ashamed. She regained her composure and said, "Nick Belt."

"That son-of-a-bitch," Louis spewed with hate in his voice. "He's going to make this right with you, Ona. I'll make sure of that."

He pulled her closer and hugged her as tight as he could. Tears rolled down her face but her secret was finally out and she felt better. Louis didn't hate her. She knew she had to tell Grams next. The look of disappointment she expected from Grams just killed her. But Louis promised he would be there for her.

"Now it's going to be okay. You need to pull yourself together and let's wipe those tears away, Sis," Louis said as he used his towel to gently wipe Leona's tears off her cheek.

"I need to see that beautiful smile of yours," he added as he pinched her cheek, "or Grams will know for sure something is up."

Chapter 37

Leona did her best to put a smile on her face as she and Louis walked to the lunch table. Gramps and the kids were already sitting and Grams said, "Well goodness gracious, it's about time. The two of you are making Gramps and these two young'uns starve. Now sit down before they all faint from hunger."

The three of them took their places alongside the others with Leona between Louis and Grams. They all joined hands and bowed their heads while Gramps said "grace."

"Bless us today, oh Lord, for the bounty we are about to receive. Thank you for the children around our table today, oh Lord, and may you keep them safe and healthy. Bless this food we are about to partake and the hands that prepared it. In Jesus name, amen."

Leona and the rest all said "amen" and she thought she felt both Louis' and Grams' hands squeeze her hands a little tighter than usual.

Later that afternoon after they had finished their lunch, Grams asked Gramps, "Would you go to the store to get some things to send home with the kids? Anna sent a list of things she needs at the farm. Why don't you take Goldie and Bud with you. Leona can stay here and help me."

Goldie grabbed the basket. She and Bud each took hold of one of Gramps' hands and they headed off with Gramps and the list.

After Gramps and the kids were out the door, Grams told Ona and Louis to help clear the table and do the dishes. Louis picked up the sweet lime pickles and deviled eggs. Ona picked up the leftover mashed potatoes and gravy while Grams grabbed the ham. Once in the kitchen, Louis looked at Leona, smiled assuredly and nodded his head towards Grams and mouthed, "You need to tell her now."

With her chin buried in her chest, Leona said, "Grams, there is something I need to tell you," as tears started to well up in her eyes.

"Oh, honey, are you okay? You know you can tell me anything." Grams looked over at Louis and he gave her a worried look.

Leona was struggling to get the words out. Each time she opened her mouth the syllables got harder and harder to come out. "I, I... um... I've done..."

Grams took hold of one of Leona's hands and led her to the kitchen chairs. They sat and Grams put her hand under Leona's chin and lifted it up so those tearful, brown eyes were looking right at her. "Honey, I know. I knew the minute you walked in the door. Your Grams' been around a long time and I know when I see a girl carrying a baby."

Leona burst into tears as Grams encircled her arms around her.

"It's going to be okay, sweetie," Grams said. Louis joined in by patting Leona on the back. Grams and Louis looked at one another shaking their heads. They really didn't know what to say but did their best to try and comfort her. The huge load was lifted and the floodgates opened up wide.

Grams was mortified but tried to be tender. She was so full of love for her granddaughter. She asked Leona about the father and what happened. Leona between sobs unveiled the happenings she had kept secret for so long. Gram's worst fears were abated when she found out the father was some boy named Nick Belt. She had always feared for Leona and Goldie after Anna married that awful Mr. Barton.

"Your mama doesn't know yet does she, Ona?" Grams asked.

"No, this is the first I have told anyone. I have been too ashamed."

"Well, honey we have to tell your mama today. Gramps and we'll take you home and be there to help you tell her. It will be okay," Grams comforted.

"And I am going to go have a talk with Nick Belt, the son of a bitch!" Louis chimed in.

"No! No! You can't, Louis!" Leona wailed.

"Now, Louis! You watch your mouth," Grams chastised. "We have to be levelheaded and do what's best for Ona right now. First we need to finish up these dishes and get ready for Gramps and the kids so we can go talk to your mama."

"I'm sorry, Grams," Louis apologized. "I'm just so mad he did this to Ona. I could break him in two."

"I know, I know, boy. My blood's boiling too but that ain't going to help or change matters. We need you to go with us when we take the kids home."

Leona rested her head on Grams' shoulder and for the first time in several weeks she started to relax and with Grams rocking her, she actually fell asleep in her arms. Louis looked at Grams' worried face and said, "Poor Sis, she's probably not slept good for days holding this all in to herself. She's exhausted. Grams just hold her and I'll clean up these dishes and go hitch up the wagon so we'll be ready when Gramps and the kids get home."

Grams nodded at her grandson—it was going to be a long day.

Chapter 38

Gramps, Grams, Louis, Leona, Goldie and Bud were all in the wagon pulled by two beautiful black horses that Gramps called Billy and Barney. They arrived at the Hendrickson/Barton farm around 3:30 in the afternoon. Louis lowered Goldie and Bud down out of the wagon and told them to run the supplies into the house for Mama. "Tell Mama that Gramps and Grams are here, too."

The kids carrying the basket no more than got to the door and Mama was flying out to greet her loving Grams and Gramps. Grams and Mama gave each other a huge hug and kiss on the cheek. Grams and Mama loved one another since the day Papa brought Mama home to meet them. They still shared that bond, even after losing a man they both loved so deeply.

Leona looked white as a ghost, afraid of what her mama was going to think and say when she found out what the others now knew. Grams had filled in Gramps with the news. Before leaving for the farm, he was able to pull Leona aside and gave her a huge hug. She smelled the smoke from his pipe tobacco on his shirt. She felt safe and protected in his arms and reassured without his saying a word.

Grams and Gramps asked Mama and Mr. Barton to go into the kitchen after they arrived. Gramps told Goldie and Bud to take the team of horses and get them some water and to brush them down. Mr. Barton was furious Louis was there and stared daggers at him when no one was looking but acted all nice in front of Gramps and Grams. Louis had his arm around Leona and they joined everybody in the kitchen. Grams asked Leona to come and sit in the chair between her mama and her. Leona was quiet and just looked down. Mama knew immediately something was wrong.

"Leona, honey, what's the matter?" Mama asked.

She couldn't speak. Grams was the one that spoke up to tell Mama and Mr. Barton what was wrong. When Grams told them the news, Mama broke down sobbing. Old man Barton was furious. Thank goodness Grams, Gramps, and Louis were there or no telling what that man would have done to Leona and Mama. Old man Barton slammed his hands down on the table and called Leona all kinds of names. He stood and before storming out of the house yelled, "I ain't having no bastard in my house."

Leona and Mama both continued sobbing and Grams tried comforting them. She looked at Gramps with a stone cold stare after Barton left. Gramps knew that look was not one to mess with. He himself was way beyond pissed. And Louis, he was writhing with anger.

That day was the beginning of the end for Mama and Mr. Barton. Things had gotten progressively worse over the previous few months because of old man Barton's drinking. Gramps smelled booze on Barton's breath when they shook hands upon arrival. The way Barton exploded at Leona's news exposed the true mean side of him. "Has Barton ever hit you, Anna?" Gramps asked Mama with a calm but stern voice.

Mama wouldn't look Gramps in the eyes. Louis was about to explode. Muttering under his breath, he turned to head out the door. Gramps grabbed his arm and said, "Louis, you need to calm down. Let me take care of this. You can come with me but don't say or do a thing."

Gramps and Louis headed outside while Grams continued to console Leona and Mama. Once outside, Gramps went to the wagon and picked up his shotgun that was under the wooden seat. Old man Barton was out in the barn. Gramps, with Louis trailing behind, walked in on Barton tipping a bottle. Pointing his shotgun at Barton, Gramps said, "You get your sorry ass on your horse and off this farm and don't ever come back again. We'll drop anything of yours, which ain't much, off at your house in town."

That was the last time Mr. Barton ever set foot on the Hendrickson farm. Later on Grams and Gramps helped Mama— without too much convincing— to divorce the mean, old drunk son of a bitch. They didn't want Anna or their grandchildren around that man. Louis moved back home and kept working in town but was able to help Mama and the kids with the farm. Gramps also came out often and offered a helping hand now that Barton was no longer around.

Once Leona's secret was out and old man Barton was gone, it was quiet on the Hendrickson farm for a few days as things were sorted out. Leona was so embarrassed but her family assured her they loved her and were there for her. Goldie and Bud were told about Leona being pregnant and they were concerned for their sister. Mama told them not to tell anyone when they went off to school the next day. "This is no one's business but ours," she said sternly.

Leona didn't go to school the rest of the week. Goldie told Mr. Hedges and Leona's classmates that Leona wasn't feeling well. Bud had a hard time not saying anything, but he knew this secret was not his to share. At home, Mama put on a strong front but actually was scared to death. She wouldn't let her little girl see her fear. "Dear God, please help me take care of my family," Mama prayed.

Louis being home brought a sense of calm. A couple of days after breaking the news to Mama about Leona's pregnancy, Louis asked Leona if she wanted to go with him fishing at the pond. She jumped at the chance. With worms on their hooks and fishing poles set, Louis and Leona sat patiently without saying a word. Before either got their first nibble, Louis in his quiet, calm voice said, "Ona, we needed to go talk to Nick and his family and get this settled."

Leona looked at him, nodded, and looked back at her fishing line dangling in the water.

"Do you want to marry him, Sis?" he asked.

Of course she said "yes." She loved Nick and knew he loved her, too. Louis promised her he would make sure Nick made this right. Nick was going to make this right one way or another. He figured time would tell.

Chapter 39

On Sunday after the secret was out, Louis hitched up Daisy, their black and white pinto horse, to the buggy and told Leona it was time to visit Nick. The Belt family had a farm outside Hale, and it would take them most of the morning to get there. There were always jokes about living in "Hell." I am going to "Hell" today. Where you from? I'm from "Hell." Right now the two siblings felt like they were going to "Hell."

The entire ride to Nick's house, Leona thought back to that night with Nick at the dance. What would he say? Why hadn't he tried to find her and talk to her? Maybe he was hurt or had gotten sick. Louis was quiet on the outside but fuming on the inside. In his mind he concocted a thousand scenarios, all of which ended with Nick on the ground with a bloody nose. Nick's last name was Belt but Louis sure wished that fellow would have learned to use one.

The siblings' anxiety rose to a heightened level upon arriving at the Belt farm. There was a really nice two-story, white house with wrap-around porch and picket fence. A couple of mangy dogs ran along the fence line barking. In the drive was a Model T car, just like the one she had dreamed Nick would pull up in and take her away from old man Barton. Leona and Louis heard Nick came from money, and from the looks of the farmstead, it was true. Louis pulled the buggy up to the hitching post and patted Leona's hand. "You stay right here. I'll go and talk to Nick and his daddy."

Leona gave Louis a half-hearted smile and watched him climb out of the buggy. He put Daisy's reins through the metal ring that was in the mouth of the black, metal horse-head hitching post outside the white gate. Louis opened the gate and the dogs barked and sniffed at his legs. They seemed to think he was okay and scampered back to the porch and laid down as Louis started the long walk to the front door.

Just as Louis was to step up on the first step, the screen door opened. Out walked a man Louis assumed was Mr. Belt. He was about the same height as Nick and looked a lot like Nick but had about 50 pounds on him. He was dressed in what appeared to be his Sunday best clothes and shined up black shoes. A cigar hung out the side of his mouth. He was definitely a man of means and quite confident in himself. Louis stopped and introduced himself holding out his hand. "Hello, Mr. Belt? I'm Louis Hendrickson. I'm from over at Havana. Clark and Anna Hendrickson are my folks. I was wondering if I could speak to your son, Nick."

No more than Louis had the words out, he saw Nick standing inside the screen door looking out. He knew there was a storm about to brew. Louis' blood was starting to boil just at the sight of Nick, and he was trying to remain calm and handle the situation like his daddy would have. Mr. Belt shook Louis' hand and smiled, "Welcome, young man. I remember meeting your daddy. He passed on a while back if I remember right. He was a good man."

"Thank you, sir. Yes, Papa was a good man."

"Just what might you need to speak to my son about?" he asked. "I'm sure anything you need to talk to him about you can share with me."

"Well sir, it's kinda personal and has to do with my sister, Leona."

"Nick, get your butt out here, now!" Mr. Belt yelled back toward the house.

The screen door creaked open and Nick slunk out of the house like a coon dog with his tail between his legs after being scolded. Mr. Belt spoke in a gruff voice, "Son, this young man here says he has something to talk to you about concerning his sister. You have any idea what this might be about?"

Nick's pale face and expression of desperation said it all. He just stuttered and said, "Nuh, uh, no sir. I don't know his sister."

Louis clinched his hands into fists and every muscle in his body tensed. "Well, sir, your boy here done got my sister pregnant, and I intend to see he does her right. She is only 16 years old," Louis said with disgust and anger in his voice staring right at Nick. "She's here in the buggy scared to death. What are you going to do about this situation?"

Mr. Belt turned and shouted at his son, "You dumb shit!" as he hauled off and smacked Nick on the back of the head. You can't keep it in your pants, can ya boy? Not another one."

Louis stood frozen on the porch. What did he mean by "another one?" Nick cowered away from his father and put his hands up to his head to protect in case another slap was coming his way. "Pa, I don't know what he is talking about. I never saw that girl before."

"Bullshit, you coward and liar," Louis bellowed as his face turned red with anger. "I saw you at the dance in Havana with my sister! I even talked to you about her at the dance in Sedan when she asked about you! She don't lie! You got her pregnant, you bastard!"

Louis' clenched fists were ready to pummel Nick when Mr. Belt stepped in. "I'm sorry, young man. It seems my poor excuse for a son has made some bad decisions. It seems he had another girlfriend in Sedan. I had a visit from her daddy. He caught Nick and his daughter out in the barn. Nick and Velma just got married in August and she's pregnant."

The revelation set Louis back. "You asshole." Nick looked down and cowered behind his father. Nick wanted to just slither away in the grass like the snake he was. Mr. Belt scowled at Nick and ordered him back in the house so he could talk to Louis. Nick turned and ran into the house like a scared little pup.

Mr. Belt puffed on his cigar and rubbed his chin as if in deep thought for a few seconds. Louis was extremely uncomfortable. He finally addressed Louis. "Son, has your sister been to a doctor? Does anyone else know about this?"

Louis said that only his mama and grandparents knew Leona was pregnant. She hadn't been to the doctor but there was no doubt she was with child. He said, "She is about five months along and she hadn't been with nobody but Nick and only one time at the dance last May. She had been too scared to say anything when she first figured out she was pregnant. We all just found out recently or we sure as hell would have been over here sooner."

Shaking his head, Mr. Belt said, "Well, damned if this ain't some pickle that boy has us in. We don't want to bring no shame down on your sister or your family or on my son's new wife and family. Shit! Shit! Shit!"

Louis could tell Mr. Belt's mind was racing and he was trying to process what Louis had just told him. Mr. Belt took another long drag on the cigar and puffed out the smoke. Finally he said, "I promise you I will take care of this. Your sister's too young to be raising a baby by herself. Ain't no way in hell my wife and my son's new wife are going to have another baby in this house. Things were bad enough before this new situation came up."

"I know, sir. We're all in a tough place," Louis chimed in getting more frustrated.

"I think the best thing for everyone would be for your sister to go away and have the baby and give it up for adoption," Mr. Belt said. "We need to talk to Doc Brown. He will be able to help us out. I will take care of everything if we can just keep this quiet."

This was not the outcome Louis had expected or even had an inkling could happen when they had headed out that morning for the Belt farm. He had envisioned they would ride in and give the news to Nick. Then Nick would invite Leona and him into the house to meet his folks and start planning a wedding.

Louis shook his head dumbfounded. Putting the baby up for adoption had not even crossed his mind. He said, "This isn't what I was expecting at all today. I figured I would come over here and be telling Nick he had to be a marrying my sister by end of the week. I don't know what to tell Leona. I'm sure she hasn't thought about anything but raising her baby with Nick. She really does love him and thought he loved her too."

"This is a damn mess, Mr. Hendrickson. I'm sorry my son was so irresponsible," Mr. Belt said.

Pausing to think over what Mr. Belt had suggested, Louis felt sick to his stomach. He finally said, "I hate to say this, but you are right, Leona is too young to have a baby and raise it by herself. I don't want her to be ashamed and bring disgrace to Mama and the family. Let me talk to Leona and Mama and see what they say. But I think this is the only way."

"Trust me on this, son. This is the best solution," Mr. Belt said. "Let me do some checking, talk to Doc Brown, and make some arrangements. Do you have any family that you could say your sister could be going away to stay with?"

Louis stopped to think about Mr. Belt's question, not totally understanding what he was implying. "Yes, I have a sister that lives in Garnett," he said. "She is married and has a couple kids. We could have her go stay with her."

"Well, she wouldn't actually stay with your sister. She would go to a home that helps girls in the family way and finds good families that want to adopt babies."

Louis thought things just seemed to go from bad to worse.

"I will get back to you in a day or two," said Mr. Belt. "You can tell everyone she is going to go and stay with your sister. This is a helluva fix my son's put us in," he added angrily. "I am sorry for the embarrassment and tell your Mama I will take care of this."

They shook hands and Mr. Belt turned and went back to the house. He climbed the steps up to the porch and opened the screen door. Turning and looking at Louis walk toward the buggy, he saw the scared girl shivering with fear. He disgustedly shook his head and walked into the house to confront his son.

Chapter 40

The walk back to the buggy was even more difficult than the walk to talk to Mr. Belt. Louis didn't have any idea how he was going to break the bad news to Leona. He thought to himself, "How do I tell her Nick was already married? It is going to break her heart."

Leona was too far from the porch to hear the conversation. She kept her head low, looking forward and not watching Louis walk to the porch. When she heard raised voices, she snuck a peek just as Mr. Belt slapped Nick. She watched helplessly as Mr. Belt and Louis yelled at Nick. She felt horrible they were so mad at Nick because of her.

Her heart skipped a beat when she saw Nick, and all those feelings for him rushed back. She wanted to be his wife and raise his baby. That would make her the happiest woman on Earth. When Nick turned and went back in the house, her heart sank. She could tell from the animated discussion and look on Louis' face as he was approaching the buggy that things had not gone well.

Louis untied the reins and climbed in the buggy with Leona. He patted her knee but didn't say a thing. He needed to calm himself before he spoke. He tapped the reins on Daisy's back and encouraged her to head for home. It was very tense and Leona was dying to know what Mr. Belt had said.

"Louis?" Leona finally whispered.

"Ona, I am so sorry but I have some bad news. It seems that asshole Nick had at least one other girlfriend and he married her. She is in the family way, too."

A shiver overtook her as the reality of what Louis said sunk in. Another girlfriend? Pregnant? Married? How could he? She was dumbstruck. Another wave of reality hit: Nick lied. He didn't love her. He must have told lots of girls the same thing. The profound hurt and embarrassment poured out of her body through sobs. Louis pulled her in to his body and hugged her. "Ona, honey, it is going to be okay. I promise."

Louis lightly tapped the reins on Daisy's back again to urge her on. He wanted to get Leona home. The ride was very quiet along the country dirt road. Leona sat transfixed, her body swayed with the motion of the buggy. They traveled through the rolling prairie grazed down by the ranchers' cattle. The grass was various shades of yellow and brown as winter was fast approaching. The closer to home, the landscape changed from rolling grasslands to small groves of trees and farmland. The leaves were either brown or had completely fallen from the trees. Leona was feeling a little like the brown grass and leaves that were dying before winter. Her life was over as she knew it. Nick was out of the picture and she was going to have a baby on her own. Life would never be the same.

As if he had read her mind, Louis whispered her name to get her attention from the far off place she seemed to be. He said a little louder, "Ona, it really is going to be okay. I spoke to Nick's dad and Mr. Belt is going to help. He wants you to give the baby up for adoption. He will pay for everything. You will just have to go away to have the baby. You can go and stay with Iva afterward."

Adoption! Leona never ever thought about the idea of giving up her baby. She was scared to death but never had adoption crossed her mind. "Louis, I can't give up my baby!"

"Sis, I know this sounds terrible. But, Ona, you are only 16. You know you can't raise a baby by yourself. Grams is too old and feeble to help you now. Mama's a mess with what she's going through with old man Barton. And think about how bad this is going to look on Mama and the family, you not married and in the family way. Think about your life and what is best for the baby. I think this is the only solution."

The rest of the way home Leona was silent and almost in a daze. True, Leona was a tough little gal but more tears trickled down her face from her crushed heart. Louis was worried this just might be too much for her to handle. But he knew Mama would be there for her when they got home and help her through this. He wasn't sure what Mama would say about giving the baby up for adoption, but he felt this was definitely the best solution. It was going to be a long couple of days as they waited for word from Mr. Belt.

Chapter 41

Anna Hendrickson waited anxiously alone all day for Leona and Louis to get back home from the Belt farm. Thankfully, Grams and Gramps had taken Goldie and Bud to town with them. Anna paced the floor and tried to keep busy cleaning the house to keep her mind off of her little girl and the trouble she had gotten into. She blamed herself for not being a better mother and for bringing the wrath of Mr. Barton upon their home. Anna was trapped between the impossible worlds of keeping a roof over her children's heads and doing what was right for them. Her thoughts raced, "What would've happened if Clark hadn't died? How could I let Mr. Barton run off my Louis? Maybe Leona wouldn't be in the fix she was in now? What are the neighbors going to think?"

With Mr. Barton gone, things were much better and she wasn't afraid anymore. Goldie and Bud were much happier than they had been in a long time, even with the concern they felt for their sister. It was so good to have Louis back home helping. It was as if the cloud hanging over the farm had been lifted. But Anna didn't know how they were going to keep the farm going. "One thing at a time," she thought. "We need to take care of Leona first."

Anna wondered what happened at the Belt farm. She pictured Leona leaving to marry and start a family of her own. How quickly her life would change with a new husband and baby. Leona marrying a strange young man that Anna had never even met before. Would he treat Leona good like Clark had treated her or would he be like Mr. Barton and make her life miserable?

As Anna's children approached the farm, they didn't know how to break the news to their mama. Leona seemed to be almost in a state of shock and was staring off at the distant fields. With one hand on the reins, Louis put his free arm again around Leona and pulled her in toward his body. He quietly said her name a couple times to bring her back to reality. She finally turned and looked at him with those lost brown eyes. The whole trip home the only thing that kept creeping into her head was the word "adoption." Louis said he thought she should give her baby up for adoption. "How could I ever do that? How could he ask me to do that?" she kept asking herself.

"Sis, I know today has been really hard on you," Louis shared. "I know you are heartbroken. When we get home, we'll have to talk to Mama and tell her what Mr. Belt said."

"Oh, Louis, I can't give my baby up for adoption. Please tell me I don't have to," she said again, tightly holding her arms across her belly and crying softly.

Louis pulled her tighter and said, "Let's talk it over with Mama and see what she thinks is best for you and the baby."

Daisy ambled down the familiar entrance from the road to the Hendrickson farm. Leona wanted to crawl into a hole and disappear like in that new book *Alice's Adventures in Wonderland* that Miss Darting read to them last year in school. When Louis stopped the buggy next to the house, he climbed out and tied Daisy's reins to the hitching post. He then helped Leona out of the buggy as she stepped down to the ground. The dogs announced their arrival and Mama ran to the door. Louis and Leona walked to the house.

Mama met them at the door and knew immediately things had not gone well. Leona was looking down. Louis looked at his mama and just shook his head with a sad frown on his face.

"Leona, why don't you go to your room and lay down. I can tell Mama about what happened," Louis said.

Leona was exhausted and couldn't face her mama. Telling her about Nick being married was too humiliating. How foolish a girl she had been to think Nick loved her. She agreed to go to her room and rest while Louis and Mama went to the kitchen and sat down at the old oak table.

"Mama, you aren't going to believe this. Nick is already married. They just got married in August and his wife is pregnant too."

Mama's jaw dropped and she wanted to scream. How could this happen? How was this boy so irresponsible and do this to her little girl? She listened as Louis reported the whole story. "Mama, Mr. Belt said Leona should give the baby up for adoption."

"Oh my no, Louis! We can't give her baby up for adoption!"

"But Mama, stop and think about this. Mr. Belt made a lot of sense. I don't want that to happen either, but we have to think about what is best for Leona and the baby. She is only 16 years old. How can she raise a baby by herself with no husband? I know we can try and help her but we can barely make ends meet now. You're already exhausted with all that's gone on with Mr. Barton. Grams' health hasn't been the greatest lately and she can't help much raising a baby at her age. And think of Leona's reputation. Who's going to marry a young girl with a baby born out of wedlock?"

Tears welled up in Mama's eyes and Louis could tell her heart was being crushed, just as Leona's had been when he mentioned the word "adoption." "Yes, I am so worried about what will happen to Leona and what everyone will say. I don't care what they say about me, but I can't bear to have them say bad things about her."

"What about the baby, Mama? What is best for the baby? Mr. Belt knows of this place for girls like Leona that's in the family way. They will take care of her until the baby is born. Then they find good homes with two parents that want to adopt a baby. I know we would love this baby but wouldn't it be better for it to have two loving parents than to be the child of a young girl and everyone look down their noses at it?"

"Louis, I know you're right, as much as it kills me to think about giving up Leona's baby and my grandchild," Mama said.

"But Louis, we can never pay for something like that."

"Mr. Belt said he would pay for everything. He would look into the details, get back to us and take care of everything. He said he wanted to save our family's good name and reputation, but I don't think he's really doing it for Leona or us. He's doing it to save face for his son-of-a-bitch boy and his family."

Mama grimaced at Louis' language and he apologized. "Mama, Mr. Belt can afford to pay for this. He has a big farm and one of those new automobiles. It looks like he has a ton of money," Louis said.

"When do we have to make a decision about this?" Anna asked sheepishly.

"He said he would contact us in a couple days. He suggested we just tell people that Leona is leaving to visit family. I told him we could tell folks that she was going to Iva's to help with her kids."

Anna held her hand flat against the side of her face and just shook her head in disbelief. Much like Leona, adoption never entered her mind. Now she was seriously thinking this was the only answer and she was going to have to talk to Leona about the fate that lay ahead. She patted Louis on his hand that was resting on the table and thanked him for being such a good son and big brother. She rose and headed to the bedroom where she found her scared, heartbroken daughter, knowing the decision that needed to be made.

Chapter 42

Early morning, February 14, 1925

The morning ritual always started with Nurse Hatson ringing the bell and waking Leona and the other girls.

"Time to get up, young ladies," she ordered in her high-pitched, shrill voice. It was the same old drill. "Get dressed, wash your faces, and comb your hair. We are to look presentable. Breakfast will be served in 15 minutes. Oh, and ladies, Happy Valentine's Day."

Leona looked over at her closest friend Dottie and rolled her eyes in disgust. Both girls pulled the covers up over their heads. Dottie's real first name was Eleanor but everyone here at The Willows called her Dottie or Dot. Leona didn't know her last name. Dottie asked Leona not to tell anyone her real name because her parents made her use a fake name to save face. Other than the headmistress, Mrs. Haworth, only Leona knew her real name. Leona told Dottie shortly after they met that she could call her Ona. She told Dottie it was the nickname her papa had given her when she was just a baby and only special people got to call her that.

Leona arrived at The Willows Maternity Sanitarium in Kansas City, Missouri, shortly before Dottie. Dot shared in a whisper with Leona about her family and her circumstances for being there. Her father was a rich lawyer in Illinois. Her parents were terribly embarrassed when she ended up pregnant and her boyfriend ran out on her. They had talked to their doctor and found out about The Willows, a home for unwed girls in the family way. Dot was whisked off by train, supposedly going to stay with her grandmother in St. Louis. Leona told Dot about her family, Nick, and Nick's father paying for her to come to this place. How it took her most of the day to ride on the Atchison, Topeka and Santa Fe train to Kansas City from Independence, Kansas.

The morning Leona was to catch the train, Louis and she left early before the sun came up to make the ride over to Independence with Mr. Belt. Mama cried, giving Leona a hug as she went out the door. Mr. Belt picked them up at their house and drove them in his Model T. It was the first time Leona ever rode in a horseless carriage. She was scared to death. It sure wasn't the car ride she had envisioned months ago with Nick taking her down Havana's main street. Her waving at her friends as they passed by.

Mr. Belt was gruff and didn't seem any too pleased. He puffed on a cigar. The nasty smoke plus the motion from riding in the back seat of the car made Leona nauseous, but she didn't throw up. She wrapped her arms tightly across her body, closed her eyes, and willed herself not to get sick. There was complete silence the whole way to the train station with Mr. Belt and Louis in the front seat and Leona alone in the back seat. Leona had wondered if Nick would come, too. She should have known he wouldn't. The trip in the Model T was the first of many traumatic experiences for Leona that day. It would be her first ride on a train and first time ever to be away from her mama and family.

When they got to the train station, Mr. Belt went to buy the tickets for Leona and Louis. Louis carried Leona's little bag while the other arm was around Leona as they walked to the train platform. Leona shivered with fear. They stood in solemn quiet as they waited for the train. Others were chatting and laughing in anticipation of the train ride but not them. When the train arrived, Mr. Belt handed Louis the tickets and nodded at Louis without saying a word. Leona kept her head down and couldn't look the man in the eyes.

Louis and Leona took those big steps up onto the train. It was quite a bit for a 16-year-old girl to take in. The conductor yelled "All aboard" and the train headed northeast toward Kansas City and Leona's new "home." Normally, one's first train ride would be exhilarating, but Leona's was petrifying. The only thing that made it tolerable was Louis' calming presence. The two sat in silence with Leona next to the window looking out but not seeing the countryside as it went by.

When the train finally arrived at the Kansas City Union Station, Mrs. Helen Lane, a nurse at The Willows, was there to meet them, just as Mr. Belt had promised. "Look for a nurse dressed in white," he had said. Nurse Lane thanked Louis for accompanying Leona and dismissed him to return home on the train. Louis sadly gave Leona one more hug and said, "Sis, all will be okay." Nurse Lane hailed a taxi, Leona's second car ride, and brought Leona to what would be her new "home" for the next several months. Louis watched the departing taxi with pain in his heart.

The Willows Maternity Sanitarium was one of several facilities established in Kansas City to help young unwed girls with child. Due to its central location and trains arriving from all directions, Kansas City was known as the adoption hub of America. The Willows opened in 1905 and young girls were sent there in seclusion to have their babies, which were then put up for adoption. Anonymity was promised and wealthy families chose The Willows, known as the "Ritz or Waldorf" of the Kansas City maternity homes, as the destination to obliterate their problem. Little did Leona know how much Mr. Belt shelled out to cover up his son's little indiscretion. The Willows was known as a highly respectable establishment and reported that only the finest young girls were allowed to stay there. They advertised as having "Bright babies ranging in ages up to 3 months of exceptional parentage of above average health and intelligence."

Leona was in a daze when the taxi stopped after the short ride. She was scared and everything was a blur. Nurse Lane was very curt and businesslike. She told Leona they had arrived at The Willows and the two got out of the taxi. Leona never forgot the long walk from the street up the steps carrying her little bag toward the ominous three-story mansion sitting on the hill. At the top of the steps that seemed to go on forever was the entrance with a beautiful wooden, columned pergola. Roses and vines blanketed the pergola providing shade in the summer and protection from the cold in the winter. But gave one an eerie feeling as if walking into a whole new world. Girls often felt as if they were walking in a tunnel as they approached the front steps. Leona never saw anything so grand in her life, not even rich banker Mr. Robertson's house in Havana could compare. The white Victorian style house had huge ornate pillars on each side of the stairs leading to the wooden door. There was a large veranda lined with pillars all the way around three sides of the building. Leona climbed the steps with Nurse Lane and entered the building, feeling completely overwhelmed in this new world. This would be Leona's "home" for the next several months.

As Nurse Hatson again rang that cursed bell for "rise and shine," Leona and Dottie knew their time under the warm covers was up. Dottie was just a few weeks older than Leona. They had become very close and were always to be found together, unless Leona was working in the kitchen. From the time Leona arrived, she was given kitchen chores to do along with several other girls. Some girls, like Dottie, didn't have to do any chores other than their laundry and keep their rooms clean. The girls who didn't have chores often snubbed those who did extra work, but Dottie never treated Leona that way. Both Leona and Dottie celebrated their December birthdays with no fanfare or cards. Leona turned

17 on December 29, 1924. It was one birthday she would never forget.

Dottie stretched and yawned. Leona slowly struggled to get her tired, swollen body out of bed. They shared a room with one other girl. There were several other rooms with girls as young as fourteen but most were older than Leona. They were all beat down with an air of undeniable sadness.

Getting dressed was always depressing. The girls wore identical maternity dresses that the girls exchanged for larger sizes as they grew. Leona pulled on her knee-high cotton lisle stockings and black, stretchy canvas shoes. The headmistress said the shoes were practical in case the girls' feet swelled. Leona's blue and white gingham dress and her new saddle shoes Mr. Belt paid for to make the train trip to Kansas City were stored in her bottom dresser drawer. These were the first clothes that weren't hand-me-downs from her sister Iva since her papa died. Head Nurse Jagger, who checked Leona in the day she arrived, told her to save them until she went home.

The headmistress, Mrs. Haworth, would make rounds and check on the girls from time to time, always dressed to the nines and was a prim and proper lady. She expected the same behavior out of the girls. The nursing staff wore white nurses' caps and starched, white bib aprons over their dresses. The Willows had a full staff of 15 to 20 nurses, as well as a cook, carpenter, engineer, housekeepers, janitor, secretary and their own pediatrician and obstetrician. Under normal circumstances, one might have thought they were in a grand hotel.

Leona had no idea how many girls were living in the house but figured there must be 20 or 30 girls. The girls seemed to be sectioned off from each other based on their arrival, three or four girls to a room. Each day the girls were checked over by one of the nurses and asked how they were feeling. The day Leona arrived she was given a complete physical and had never been so humiliated in her whole life as she was poked and prodded by complete strangers. Besides being checked over daily by the nurses, the girls were taken to the massage room where they were given several types of massages to prevent "stretch marks" and to aid in labor and delivery. The Willows' ads bragged that the young women often left The Willows with no marks or signs to indicate they had ever given birth.

On this cold February morning, Leona and Dot washed their faces in the bathroom and combed their hair. They could hear the wind blowing outside and were thankful for the warmth of their home away from home. The girls headed downstairs from the dormitory to the dining hall for breakfast. Leona and Dot walked arm-in-arm as they were the last two girls to reach the bottom of the stairs. They noticed a couple of new girls who looked shell-shocked and they totally sympathized in a way only they could.

Breakfast was typically lumpy oatmeal with toast and a hard-boiled egg. The girls were each to drink a glass of fresh cow's milk. Dot hated milk and it was a real chore for her to down a full glass. On occasion, the girls found boxes with a funny looking rooster on it. Leona had never had cornflakes before coming to this place. She did like them but thought it sure was strange to get food from a box.

This morning The Willow's cook, Mrs. Welbourne, carried in a platter stacked high with pancakes. The girls screamed with excitement. "Hush, hush now girls or I will just have to take these outside and feed the dogs," chided Mrs. Welbourne.

The girls were amazed that Mrs. Welbourne took the time to make heart-shaped, Valentine's Day pancakes for the girls! The smell of the maple syrup was torturous as each girl waited her turn for the syrup and homemade butter to make their way around the table. Leona and Dottie ate until they were stuffed. The pancakes were delicious. They still got their hard-boiled eggs. Leona thought if she lived to be 80 years old, she would never eat another hard-boiled egg.

After breakfast, the girls were sent back to their rooms or could go to the impressive library to find something to read. The two girls whose turn it was to do dishes started clearing the table. Leona and Dot meandered into the library where a fire was burning in the fireplace. They were allowed an hour to let their breakfast settle before starting chores or being checked over by the staff. The girls read, played cards or dominoes, or looked at the same old raggedy magazines that were donated to The Willows by Mrs. Haworth and the nursing staff. Among them were old *Life* magazines. Leona looked at the drawings over and over of the beautiful places and people, dreaming of a whole different world. This was her only escape since the girls never were allowed to leave the facility.

Dominoes was Leona's favorite game, and she and Dottie would almost always be playing at the little game table. Today though Leona just didn't feel like playing. She was tired, her back hurt and was just terribly uncomfortable. She sat in the big overstuffed, red high-backed chair close to the fire and closed her eyes. She thought back to a simpler time. She thought of her mama and papa and the farm. She could see Mama with Iva, Louis, Goldie, and Bud all sitting around the table sharing dinner with Grams and Gramps.

An image came to mind of a very handsome, young man with dark brown hair. She wondered what Nick was doing. It had been over three months since she last saw him. As she drifted out of consciousness with the heat from the fire warming her body, she danced with Nick in her dreams.

Chapter 43

Leona woke from her dream to hear Nurse Hatson say it was time for the girls to go their rooms to tidy up and take naps while they awaited their "inspection." Just as she reached the top of the stairs, Leona felt a sharp pain and then heard a shriek. It was Dottie. "Ona! Your water broke."

Leona and Dottie made their way back down the stairs to find Nurse Hatson. She was very calm and told the girls all would be just fine. She ushered the girls into the confinement chamber where the girls were placed while in labor. Dottie helped Leona change into an open-backed gown and crawl into the bed then Nurse Hatson told Dottie to leave. She begged to stay with her friend, but Nurse Hatson curtly said, "No, Dot. It is time for you to leave. Go back to your room."

Nurse Jagger arrived and found Leona having small contractions. She sent Nurse Hatson to inform Dr. Kepner, the house obstetrician, that Leona was in labor. Leona was never so scared in her whole life. She just knew she was going to die. Nurse Jagger tried to comfort her though her demeanor matched the sterile room. All Leona could think of was how badly she wanted her mama to be there holding her hand and telling her everything would be okay.

Nurse Hatson fetched the doctor from his office, which was not too far from the confinement chamber. Dr. John W. Kepner had been the Willow's well-respected doctor since the sanitarium's conception in 1905. He had delivered more babies than he could remember. "Hi, Nurse Jagger, how's my little Ona doing?" he said as he came into the room.

Dr. Kepner gave Leona her first physical the day she arrived and examined Leona at least twice a week. He said she was as healthy as a horse. With so many girls, he developed only professional medical relationships. But Leona was different. There was something about this sweet, sad country girl that tugged at his heartstrings. He knew she wasn't quite from the "wealthy" stock most of the girls were at the Willows. When the doctor met Leona that difficult first day, he asked her name. "My name is Leona," she said barely above a whisper. "My papa had called me Ona, but he has passed on."

"What a beautiful name," Dr. Kepner said.

Leona looked up at the doctor and said shyly, "You remind me of my papa. Would you like to call me Ona?"

"I would be honored to call you Ona." From that time on, they had a special bond and Leona was always happy to see the doctor when he came to check her and the baby.

The doctor walked up beside Leona's bedside and took her hand and squeezed it. Doc said, "Happy Valentine's Day, Ona. I guess it's time."

Leona looked at him, trying to smile, but even with her tough-as-nails act, Dr. Kepner knew she was scared.

"Now Ona, don't you be scared. You know I won't let anything happen to you or the baby. All is going to be just fine."

He asked, "How often are the contractions?"

"About every fifteen minutes now," Nurse Jagger said.

Just then Leona let out a cry and squeezed Dr. Kepner's hand tightly. "You still have that strong farm girl grip there, young lady," he said with a laugh.

After examining Leona, he said all was coming along nicely. She was dilated 5 centimeters. "Ona, it is going to be a little bit longer before you're ready to deliver so try and stay calm and do not push," Dr. Kepner said, emphasizing *do not*.

Leona just wanted it to be over with. She was a thin gal and her belly had gotten fairly good sized. Dr. Kepner figured she was going to have a pretty big baby and it might be a tough delivery. If they had any complications, girls were rushed to the nearby hospital but he hoped that wouldn't be necessary with Leona. He told Nurse Jagger it was probably going to be a few hours before Leona was ready to deliver.

"Ona, you're doing great. The baby isn't quite ready to come into this world so I am going to go check on the other girls, but Nurse Hatson will come get me if things progress faster than I expect."

He again squeezed her hand. "Thank you, Doc," she said.

After the doctor left, Nurses Jagger and Hatson took turns with the other nurses always having someone staying with Leona. Time drug by and Leona was so miserable. She was sweating and had chills it seemed all at the same time. The nurse dabbed her head with damp cloths, mopping up the sweat on her brow. Leona just wanted to scream and have this nightmare experience over. But she followed Dr. Kepner's orders and didn't push even though she wanted to so badly.

Chapter 44

Evening, February 14, 1925

"Push, Leona, push."

Leona was pushing with all her might and screamed in pain.

"Okay, stop pushing, Ona," Dr. Kepner said. "Take a couple deep breaths."

Dr. Kepner came back a couple of times over the next few hours and checked on Leona. At 6:00 p.m. she still wasn't quite ready to deliver but was close enough he decided to stay and not go home for supper. He asked the cook, Mrs. Welbourne, to fix him a plate. Another two hours passed. Leona was in her seventh hour of labor.

Nurses Jagger and Hatson went home and were replaced by Nurses Wicker and White. Nurse Wicker brought the hot boiled towels the doctor asked her to fetch when he came back from supper. Nurse White stayed by Leona's bedside. Dr. Kepner encouraged Leona to breathe and to push when contractions hit. The pain was so intense she thought she would pass out. At one point, she hoped she would. "Ona, I can see the baby's head," Dr. Kepner said excitedly. "There are the shoulders, push again, Ona."

Leona gritted her teeth and pushed.

"It's almost here, honey," Nurse White encouraged Leona.

"Just one more time, Leona," Doc said.

Leona took one more deep breath and pushed with all her might. She swore she felt her bones move. Another excruciating bolt of pain shot through her body and she screamed.

Doc rejoiced, "Alleluia, it's a beautiful baby girl."

He looked up at the big clock on wall and said, "Born at 7:55 p.m."

Next thing Leona heard was the sound of a hand slap flesh and a small cough. The cough turned into a huge cry, and she realized that cry was her baby girl. Nurse Wicker took the baby from the doctor, wiped her clean, and wrapped her in a blanket. Leona was exhausted but asked to see her baby. Nurse White said the baby was beautiful with ten fingers and ten toes and just a little dark brown hair on her head. Dr. Kepner walked up to Leona and wiped her sweaty brow and said, "I am so proud of you, Ona."

Nurse Wicker placed the baby girl in Leona's arms and tears streamed down Leona's face. Her beautiful baby girl! The sweetest Valentine's Day present anyone could ever receive. At the time, she had no way of knowing it would become her least favorite holiday.

Nurses Wicker and White encouraged Leona to allow the baby to nurse and helped as needed. The baby was quite strong and alert and quickly took to nursing. Nurse Wicker then said, "You need your rest, Leona. We will take the baby to the nursery until time to nurse again."

Though she was exhausted and her body hurt, the removal of her baby from her arms made her feel so empty. But she eventually drifted off to sleep as a new chapter in her life was soon to begin.

Leona remained in the confinement chamber for a couple days to recuperate. During this time she only was allowed to see the nurses, Dr. Kepner and her baby, which would be brought in just for feeding every few hours. By the third day, Leona was so sick of the white sterile walls and desperately wanted out of there. Her highs and lows were at a fevered pitch. Highs when her baby was brought to her and lows when she sat for hours alone with maybe a book to read when not sleeping or staring off into space.

On the fourth day, Leona was allowed to go back to a room but not to the room she shared with Dot. Leona was in a room by herself and all her belongings had been moved to this room. She had her meals with other girls that had delivered their babies and was not allowed to socialize with the girls who were still pregnant. They were to stay in their rooms to rest and only were allowed to go to a small dining room for meals. Another three days passed before Leona saw Dot again. The two met in the small dining hall and hugged. Dot gave birth just three days after Leona. They were under the watchful eye of the nurses and weren't allowed to share much about their birthing experiences. They did exchange that Leona had a girl and Dot had a boy.

In her solitary room for the next week, Leona would have her baby girl brought to her by one of the nurses. After feeding, her baby was taken back to the nursery with the other babies.

Mrs. Lowe, assistant superintendent of The Willows, sat in the white cane-backed chair beside Leona's bed while Leona nursed her baby. Leona grinned from ear to ear looking down at her beautiful baby doll. Mrs. Lowe watched for a little while and then cleared her throat and quietly said, "Leona?"

Leona looked up at the stern-faced Mrs. Lowe who asked, "Do you remember what was said about the baby when you arrived here at The Willows?"

Leona's smile faded. She looked away and back at her baby. Quietly Leona muttered, "Yes, ma'am."

"Good, you must keep what I said in mind."

One more time even quieter, "Yes, ma'am."

"Have you picked out a name for the baby? We need a name to put on the birth certificate for the adoption."

Leona's smile returned as she looked longingly at her beautiful baby. She spent many hours since arriving at The Willows thinking about a name for her baby. She had chosen the name Louis if the baby had been a boy. A name for a girl was more difficult. After much deliberation, it wasn't until she saw her baby girl that she chose a name.

"Her name is Marcia."

February 24, 1925

Leona held Marcia in her arms and the baby was nursing. She was rocking her gently and humming a song. She was such a beautiful little baby. Her little hand was wrapped around Leona's finger and held tight as she nursed. Leona was so proud of her little girl and she could actually see her papa in Marcia's eyes. Just then Nurse Jagger and a man she had remembered seeing before came into her room.

"Hi Leona, do you remember Dr. Stewart?"

Of course, Leona remembered him. He was the man that poked a needle in her arm and took blood when she first arrived. That hurt so bad. "Yes, ma'am."

"Dr. Stewart is here again to do a test to make sure you and your baby are healthy. He will draw a little blood. We will know the results in a couple days."

The thought of the needle made her cringe but even worse was him pricking her baby. Leona went first and he put the needle in her arm to draw the blood. Then while she held Marcia tightly, the doctor poked her baby's tiny heel, and she started to cry. It broke Leona's heart every time her baby cried. It didn't take long, and she was able to quiet the baby quickly. Leona rocked Marcia while she nursed. The newborn drifted off to sleep. Leona loved holding her baby girl in her arms, but the nurse took Marcia away from her and back to the nursery. Leona knew their days together were numbered.

Chapter 45

March 25, 1925

The Union Pacific train whistle blew as the slow-moving passenger car traveled through the northeast Kansas countryside. Inside Emma gently rocked back and forth. Though it wasn't her first train ride to Kansas City, she was a little nervous riding by herself.

She thought back to her husband and the little farm she left just a few hours ago. Lynn, her husband of eleven years, took her to the tiny train depot in Delia in their buggy. The trip took a little more than two hours. It was a long six-mile ride so they left before the sun peeked over the horizon. Before leaving, Emma crept into her two sleeping boys' bedroom. Quiet and sensitive Philip was five and a half years old. Inquisitive and ornery John Vernon would be four in June. She gave each a peck on his cheek before she left the house.

Lynn's Aunt Winnie would be staying to watch the boys. Emma knew they would be in good hands, and in John Vernon's case, strong hands. She didn't need to worry. Emma rested her head against the clear window while reflecting on her life and today, which was going to shape the rest of her family's lives.

Emma Mullinix Keller was a proud, quiet, tenderhearted farm wife. She loved the farm that she and Lynn were working on to build into a respectable place. It meant many sacrifices. She hadn't worn a new dress since young Phillip came into their lives.

Life for Emma had not been easy. Her parents were Flora Bell and Elijah. She didn't remember her father, as he died before

Emma's first birthday. He died April 17, 1890, from the fever that took so many, including her baby brother who died three years earlier on the exact same date. Emma's mama lovingly referred to her husband Elijah as E.J. Some people called him Romey. When Emma asked about him, Flora Bell couldn't, or wouldn't, tell her much about her papa or her baby brother.

Though Emma knew her father's name, he was a mystery. She didn't know if he had any living family left. The little farm they lived on was north of Delia, Kansas, and was Elijah's place. He bought it before marrying Flora Bell, and she and Emma inherited it. When Emma asked where her father came from, her mother said he always told her "I slid down the tail of a cow." Not knowing much about her father left an empty spot in Emma's heart that she felt could never be filled.

When her mother remarried, life for Emma was never the same. Flora Bell married a man named Ralph Waldo Bahner when Emma was about five years old. He was a very smart and godly man but never wanted a stepdaughter. He treated Emma as if she didn't exist, ignoring her unless she was crying or whining and he would tell her to be quiet. He looked at Emma and was reminded of the man he was afraid was Flora Bell's true love. Flora Bell loved her new husband but she didn't know how to get him to love her daughter.

One day Flora Bell found Emma in the middle of the cattle pen where she had wandered trying to follow Ralph. He just ignored Emma and left her stranded in the cow pen crying. Flora Bell ran to her scared little girl, scooped her up and carried her to safety. She knew this wasn't going to work and with a heavy heart, packed Emma's clothes and hitched the buggy.

Fortunately, Flora Bell's parents, John and Katherine Ward, lived just a few miles away from her farm. Katherine loved her little granddaughter and brought Emma into her house with open arms away from her new son-in-law's indifference. Emma spent her early years living with them, and Grandma Ward had a huge impact on making Emma the woman she became.

Emma considered herself a tomboy and would always rather be outdoors doing chores with Grandpa than spending time in the kitchen. Even still, her grandmother was an excellent cook and shared her skills with her granddaughter. Emma recalled how many times Grandma woke her before the sun had risen to help make yummy lard crust fruit pies. Apple, of course, was her favorite.

Emma loved riding her pony when she wasn't busy helping her grandparents. She loved playing the piano as well. She took piano and organ lessons from a neighbor lady, Miss Evans, who later became the wife of Jess Willard, the 1915 heavyweight boxing champion of the world. The Wards also provided room and board for many of the local school teachers. Miss May Lockmiller taught Emma to embroider, tat, knit, and crochet. Grandma Ward taught Emma how to quilt and piece quilts. But most importantly, Grandma Ward instilled the deep Christian faith that gave Emma her strength.

When Emma met Lynn Keller, it was love at first sight. She knew she wanted to spend the rest of her life with this man. He was tall and handsome and his thick, dark hair and sparkling blue eyes gave her goose bumps. Lynn's quiet demeanor held a mystery that transformed Emma from a self-assured, young woman into a blushing schoolgirl.

Lynn didn't win her over with his words, there weren't many. Nor was money a factor, he had none. It was his steady-as-a-rock, self-assured manner and confidence that stole Emma's heart and won her devotion. His quiet nature would always hold a spell over her. He never had to say he loved her to know just how deeply he did. As she reflected on their love, she wondered if this was what her own mother had loved about Emma's mysterious father, Elijah.

Chapter 46

As the train slowly made its way east toward Kansas City, Emma gazed out the window and saw the morning sun lighting up the prairie and fields along the railroad track. Patches of snow in the ditches were hidden from the sun, keeping the snow from melting. It brought back the day she pledged her love to Lynn. She remembered the snow-lined ditches and the brisk air, even though the sun was shining brightly that day, March 4, 1914.

Emma recalled she and Lynn boarded his spring wagon and headed for Holton, Kansas. Lynn's younger brother, Levi, and Emma's best friend, Gladys King, went along to stand up for them. With reins in Lynn's hands, he and Levi sat in the front seat and didn't say much on the trip. Snuggling close under the lap blanket that she had quilted, Emma and Gladys kept each other warm. They whispered and giggled with excitement.

The ceremony was performed by Reverend S. A. Fulton, a Presbyterian minister. It was simple and quick but meant as much to Emma as if she was married in the beautiful, red brick Presbyterian Church in Rossville, Kansas, with the stained-glass windows she visited once with Grandma Ward. She dreamed of a wedding in that church but her wedding day had been perfect. After the simple ceremony, there was no time or money for a honeymoon. It took the whole day to ride to Holton and back. Chores were waiting.

Family was everything for Emma and Lynn. Riding by herself on the train, though excited about what lie ahead, she missed everyone back home. She thought about the difference between their families. Lynn had a huge family and was very close to his seven brothers and sisters, especially his twin sister, Lilly. Their parents named them Lindsay Vance and Lillian Blanche.

Emma adored her in-laws. Lynn's father, Alfred, and mother, Celestia, were married in 1876 and first lived in Abilene, Kansas. In fact, one of their acquaintances was Wild Bill Hickock, a deputy sheriff at that time. They moved several times eventually settling in the Delia-Adrian communities. Alfred died shortly after Lynn and Emma were married, but Lynn's mother lived a good, long life and loved Emma as her own. Lynn's brother, John, and his wife, Winnie, were especially close to Lynn and Emma. Emma always found it ironic that Lynn's grandfather's name was Flora, just like her mother's first name. Thankfully he didn't have the middle name "Bell."

Emma's mama, Flora Bell, and Mr. Bahner had six children so Emma had three half-brothers and three half-sisters, but they weren't very close. Even with her loving Grandma and Grandpa Ward pouring their love out to Emma, she always felt a void that she was not a real part of her mother's family. Flora Bell and Mr. Bahner moved to Lexington, Oklahoma, and started a new life there shortly after Emma went to live with the Wards. They had always kept in touch and she loved her siblings, but they weren't a close-knit family like the Kellers.

After getting married, Emma and Lynn lived with Grandma Ward. Grandpa Ward died January 1, 1914 before Lynn and Emma were married. Lynn helped Grandma Ward to keep the farm going. That same year, Emma's stepfather approached her with an offer to buy out her share of the Mullinix farm. It was hard for Emma to give up the only connection she had with her papa. But she and Lynn discussed it and sold Mr. Bahner her share of the 80 acres. This became the seed money Lynn and Emma used to start the process of buying a little 40 acre farm on the Potawatomie Indian Reservation and fulfill their dream of having their own place.

Family being so important to Emma, she wanted to give Lynn children and start a family of their own. Lynn never said as much, but she knew it was important to him as well. They'd been married for about four years, but the babies never came. Emma's best friend, Elizabeth, already had two children.

One summer day Emma was at the quilting circle that she helped establish before she was married. It was called the Merry-Go-Round Club. Over many years, this club was a regular social meeting place for the local women, both family and friends. Emma taught many young women all the crafts she learned from Grandma Ward and other family members and friends. These women kept their friendship alive by getting together to stitch beautiful quilts. It was so much fun and faster to finish a quilt with all their hands working together.

The group gathered at Aunt Maude Thompson's house as usual. Aunt Maude really wasn't Lynn or Emma's real aunt. Maude's husband, Chris, was a brother to Nels and Ludwig Thompson who married Lynn's sisters, Alta and Ella Keller. So Emma and Maude really weren't blood related, but she lovingly called her Aunt Maude. Aunt Maude was the best quilter in the county.

Young Bertha was sitting next to Emma. Bertha was one of Lynn's cousins. She was few years younger than the other women sewing. She was a big girl and didn't have much of a filter when it came to what she had to say. She looked Emma in the eye and asked, "Emma, when you and Mr. Keller going to have a baby?"

Aunt Maude gasped at the girl's boldness and told Bertha to hush. Emma turned red in the face with embarrassment. Best friend Elizabeth chimed in quickly and said, "The good Lord hasn't decided yet and when it is time, it will be time."

Not another word was said for a couple minutes while the ladies worked in silence until Aunt Maude announced, "I think it's time for some refreshments. Who wants some lemonade?"

Chapter 47

On days of the quilting circle, Emma always drove the buggy and picked up Elizabeth at her house. On the way home this day, Elizabeth put her arm around Emma to comfort her friend as she could see how the rude comment hurt her.

Elizabeth and Emma were close ever since Elizabeth married Lynn's good friend, Howard Houck. She wasn't raised in these parts. In fact, Elizabeth was raised a city girl and even attended college. She met Howard while visiting family and fell head over heels for him. They married after just knowing each other for a few weeks and started a whole new way of life. If it hadn't been for Emma, Elizabeth always said she wouldn't have survived. Emma taught her how to bake bread, sew a new dress, and even how to clean a chicken. They became like sisters.

"Emma dear, I know how bad you want to give Lynn a baby," Elizabeth said. "Please don't be mad at me, but have you ever thought about adopting?"

"Adopting?" That had never ever crossed Emma's mind as an option and she sat in a daze.

Elizabeth went on. "Emma, I don't know if you know it but there are some places in big cities where they have babies that need a home because their mothers are young and can't take care of them. I know of a place in Kansas City. Think about it and see what Lynn would say about you adopting a baby. You have so much love to give and I know you and Lynn would make great parents."

The idea spun in Emma's head. She had never thought about adopting. It just wasn't something people in these parts did, taking in some stranger's baby. I mean, families all the time raised another family member's child, like Grandma Ward took her in, but not a stranger's baby. Emma knew what it felt like to not be wanted. She carried this sadness plus not feeling a real part of her mama's new family. Even though she was blessed having Grandma and Grandpa Ward, there was always an emptiness in Emma's heart that she couldn't deny. The feeling of not being wanted was probably part of the appeal of Elizabeth's idea of adopting. There were unwanted babies that needed love and she had love to give.

But what would Lynn say? Would he think it was a crazy idea? Would he be able to love someone else's baby or be like her stepfather? It was a long ride the rest of the way home to Grandma Ward's after dropping off Elizabeth.

Several days passed and Emma's mind seldom wandered away from Elizabeth's suggestion of adopting a baby. It scared her but also warmed her heart to think there might be a baby out there that needed her and Lynn's love. She wrestled with the idea for days and slept fitfully.

One day Emma broached Grandma Ward with the idea of adopting a baby and she offered sage advice. "Emma, you have such a huge heart and you need to share it. There's lots of babies out there needin' a good home like you could give'em. I know that Lynn would love that baby like his own just like you would, and you need children when you two get your own farm going. The good Lord willing, you can be the momma to some baby that needs you. Talk to your husband and see what he says."

Emma mustered up the courage to talk to Lynn. One night after supper, Lynn lit his pipe and read a book by the light of the coal oil lamp. After she washed and dried the supper dishes, Emma sat next to Lynn in her rocker and picked up her crocheting needles and yarn. Before she could get a word out,

Lynn looked at her and said, "Emma, you ready to tell me what you've been thinking about so hard the past few days?"

She smiled and loved that he knew her so well. "Well, I've been thinking about something Elizabeth said to me the other day," she said. "We were talking about that we've been married for four years and the good Lord don't seem to be ready for us to have any children and maybe we won't ever. I was wondering if you had ever thought about adopting a baby for us to love and raise as our own."

She paused to see what his reaction was. When he didn't show any signs of emotion, she began talking faster and faster as if she only had a few seconds to get this out and persuade this man she loved to agree. She rambled, "I know it's kind of a crazy idea but you would be such a great father. You are going to need help running the farm we are going to have one day. I would so love to have a baby. And...,"

Lynn reached and took her hand in one of his calloused farm hands and pulled the pipe from his lips and said, "Shush now, slow down there."

She tried to read his face. As usual, there was no decoding what this man was thinking with his stoic facial expression, even though his eyes had a hint of sparkle. With his typical pause and deliberate way of first thinking before saying exactly what he wanted to say, Lynn stated, "If that is what you want, I think it is a great idea."

The look on her face was priceless. Emma put her arms around him and gave him a huge hug and kiss. She was beyond elated. Lynn gave her his wry little grin and mischievous look. The question hadn't caught Lynn off guard because he knew Emma was talking to Grandma Ward about adopting a baby. Grandma Ward primed the pump so to speak. She knew Lynn well enough to know that he would need time to think about this and wanted him to be prepared when Emma asked so he would say yes. Lynn knew how badly Emma wanted a child. He had to admit that he also longed for a son or daughter. So he was just waiting for Emma to bring up the question. He already knew the answer.

Chapter 48

Emma stayed up late several nights writing and rewriting her letter to the home in Kansas City for unwed mothers Elizabeth told her about. Elizabeth had seen advertisements in the paper for a place called The Willows Maternity Sanitarium that had healthy babies from good families for adoption.

The coal oil lamp flickered as Emma labored over just the right words to say. Her letter told all about her and Lynn and their families. She shared that they lived with Grandma Ward to help run the farm. She told about the little farm they had bought and planned to move to soon. They first bought the small, four-room house with about 40 acres of land. It was perfect for raising a family and they were adding more land as they could afford.

The little farm that Lynn and Emma used her inheritance money to purchase was on the Potawatomi Indian Reservation and owned by Native Americans who, after the Allotment Act of 1887, were allowed to sell their land. These Native American owners weren't farmers and wanted to sell the land to move to the city. Lynn treasured the papers he was given that were signed by President Woodrow Wilson on November 5, 1914, giving the indians permission to sell the land to the Kellers. Eventually, these documents were passed on to daughter Wanda with a note from Lynn saying, "Keep these important papers, they might be worth something one day."

Lynn looked the land over well. The dark, deep clay soil was heavy and well suited for crops. A small creek quietly meandered through the middle of the place when there wasn't a gully washer.

The south section was a steep hill with huge quartzite rocks jutting out that were left from the remains of glaciers thousands of years earlier. It also was covered with big trees ideal for protecting cattle in brutal Kansas winters. The north section was rolling hills perfect for pastureland or to plow and plant wheat. The small, four-room house was located on a hill on the western edge along the road. It faced south overlooking the valley. Lynn told Emma he knew this was the place for them to raise a family

Emma loved the farm as well and the fact it was only about five miles as the crow flies to Grandma Ward's house didn't hurt one bit. It also was just a little over two miles straight east of her best friend Elizabeth's place. The Kellers' and Houcks' long, loving friendship lasted well over 60 years. The highlight each year was the Houck Picnic hosted in August by Howard and Elizabeth. Originally called the "Club Girl" picnic, it was started as a way for the quilting gals to get together with family and friends but became a community tradition as a time for old friends to reunite and share food and friendship.

After Emma and Lynn made the decision to adopt, Emma decided to ask for a boy for Lynn. In her letter, she described Lynn and the love he had to give a child. She explained that they had been married for four years but had not been blessed with a child and wanted to expand their family. She told how she would love and take care of a baby if she was just given the chance. The letter told of their Christian beliefs and how they were God-fearing people. She played the piano at the little Adrian and Mount Olive churches and taught Sunday school.

After reading and rereading the letter several times, Emma signed her name and showed the letter to Lynn. He read it carefully and smiled before signing as well. She folded the letter neatly, put it in the envelope, and sealed it with a kiss. Emma asked Doc Miller to write a reference letter for Lynn and her. Grandma Ward and Elizabeth each wrote one as well, telling what a wonderful mother Emma would be. The next day Emma went to town with Grandma Ward and mailed her letter.

Several agonizing weeks passed. The long, hot summer days were busy though with shocking wheat and putting up hay. It helped keep her mind off the thoughts of adoption and fear that she and Lynn would be turned down as suitable parents. Just as she was about to give up hope, a letter arrived with word from The Willows Maternity Sanitarium. It stated the Kellers were approved as fit parents and were officially added to the waiting list.

After a few more long months of waiting, the Kellers' prayers were answered in January of 1920. A baby boy was born October 8, 1919, and available for them to adopt. Emma and Lynn boarded the train to Kansas City to pick up their new son. Aunt Winnie went along with them for support because Emma was a nervous wreck about bringing the baby home on the train with just Lynn.

Arriving in Kansas City at Union Station, Emma and Lynn were extremely anxious though Lynn remained calm on the outside. They weren't used to a big city like this. They were glad Aunt Winnie was with them as she was more worldly, having traveled some with Uncle John. As stated in their letter, they were to take a taxi to The Willows Maternity Sanitarium at 2929 Main Street, just a few blocks from the train station. The massive train station was the most beautiful thing Emma had ever seen in her life. The hustle and bustle of all the people running to catch trains or meeting loved ones was overwhelming. Emma happened to notice a sad young woman that was crying while sitting on a bench waiting for a train. She couldn't help but wonder if this could be a young mother who just left her baby for adoption.

Aunt Winnie helped guide the young couple outside to where there were taxis in a line to pick up passengers. She told Lynn to tell a driver where they needed to go and ask if he would take them. The driver was more than happy to take them the short distance and the three climbed into the taxi with Lynn up front. Emma was in a daze. The short ride to The Willows took just a couple minutes and the taxi driver pulled over to the sidewalk, got out, and opened the doors for Emma and Aunt Winnie. Lynn paid the driver the small fare and joined the two on the sidewalk. They were in stunned amazement as they looked up at the huge mansion on the hill. "Are you sure this is the right address?" Lynn asked the driver before he got back in his taxi.

"Yes, sir. This is The Willows," the driver said with authority as if he had made the run many a time.

The Willows was like nothing Emma or Lynn had seen before. Aunt Winnie, of course from her travels, had seen large buildings but had to admit this was quite the facility with its pillars and beautiful landscaping. "Well, we didn't come here to gawk at some building," Aunt Winnie said. "Let's go get your son."

The three made the long trek up the hill to the front door. They rang the bell and a woman dressed in all white with a nurse's cap answered the door. They introduced themselves as the Kellers and were there to pick up their baby. The nurse escorted them to a parlor that was as nicely decorated as anything Emma had seen. They sat nervously until a well-dressed woman came in the room and introduced herself as Mrs. Maudene Lowe, assistant superintendent. She welcomed them and said they needed to do some paperwork. She presented lots of papers that Lynn and Emma would need to sign, explaining they would be legal guardians of the baby until the adoption was finalized, that is if they decided to adopt the baby.

Mrs. Lowe rang for a nurse and asked her to bring the baby to the room. The nurse left and returned carrying a baby wrapped in a blanket. He was introduced as baby Timothy and was just over three months old. Mrs. Lowe said his mother was a very healthy, pleasant farm girl and his father was a farm boy. The nurse placed the baby in Emma's arms. She fell in love at first sight. Mrs. Lowe asked, "Now if you would like, we can show you another baby boy?"

Emma looked at Lynn. The smile on Lynn's face told her all she need to know. "No, this baby will be just perfect."

Aunt Winnie held the baby while the paper work was all signed. The nurse provided all the baby's needs (bottles with cow's milk, cloth diapers, etc.) for the trip home and Emma put them all in the small bag she had brought with her. Mrs. Lowe hailed a taxi for the four and they were taken back to Union Station to head for home and began a new journey. All the way home Emma held their new son. They both knew they had made the right decision. Lynn and Emma had already chosen a name for their new son, Philip Wayne Keller. What a joyful way to start the new year.

That spring, Emma and Lynn moved to their little farm and new home with baby Philip. It was not too long after they settled into their new life and routine and "surprise," as often happens when a young couple adopts, Emma found out she was pregnant. A double blessing from the Lord. John Vernon Keller came into the world June 19, 1921.

Chapter 49

♡♡

March 25, 1925

Emma was on the train once again heading to Kansas City. Emma held in her hand the cream-colored envelope that arrived just two days earlier. The train rattled on in its steady pace with a few stops along the way for more passengers to board. Four years had passed since the day John Vernon had joined her little family of Lynn and Philip. Lynn and Emma had hoped to have more children, but it didn't seem to be in the good Lord's plans. Emma didn't understand why they didn't have another baby after John Vernon. When Emma approached Lynn about the idea of adopting another baby, he didn't hesitate and said yes.

Her two boys were now home in their bed with Aunt Winnie watching over them and she wondered what new bundle of joy awaited her in Kansas City. She took the letter out of the envelope and read it again. She thought back just two days earlier when the letter arrived. Emma knew immediately who sent it. The familiar logo and fancy handwriting were on the envelope they received five years earlier.

Upon its arrival, the envelope sat unopened on Lynn's oak desk. All day Emma was having trouble focusing on anything but the letter. While making supper, Emma stirred the brown gravy to go with the potatoes that were boiling on the wood stove. Countless times she looked over at the letter wanting to go open it. What if it was a rejection? No, she would wait for Lynn. She said a little prayer and asked for strength to be patient and for good news.

John Vernon came in from the porch. He was barefooted and had that mischievous look on his face that always meant he was about to get into trouble. It was Lynn's sly smile. Even though it was only March, the weather had been warmer than usual the past couple of weeks and the boys refused to wear their old shoes. Philip's shoes were hand-me-downs from cousin Charlie. Poor little John Vernon's worn shoes had already endured Charlie and Philip.

John Vernon edged over to the desk and reached for the letter. "Don't you dare, John Vernon!" chided Emma.

It was a tone John Vernon was not accustomed to hearing. The few times it touched his ears, he learned to pay attention. He climbed down from the chair that was pushed up to Pa's desk. Head down, he stealthily walked over to Ma at the stove and tugged on her long, gray everyday dress. Emma picked him up and gave him a peck on the cheek and big hug.

"I am sorry, Ma. What's that funny paper?" the beautiful little boy with the big, brown, begging-forgiveness eyes asked.

"Nothing, boy," she replied, "just something for me and your Pa. Now go out and fetch your Pa and Philip for supper."

"Yessum, Ma."

As the boy headed out the door, she glanced at the envelope one more time and forced herself to tend to her gravy and the task of feeding her family.

That evening Lynn was resting in the rocker after the long day's work. Supper was another good meal but he did notice the brown gravy was kind of lumpy, a telltale sign Emma's mind was somewhere else. He had no doubt what it was. Philip asked him earlier when they were washing up for supper, "What's that letter that's got Ma so cranky, Pa?"

Philip never got his answer. "You never mind, boy," was all his father said. Lynn never spent much time talking unless it was something he felt needed to be discussed and always in his own good time.

Emma had just finished up the dishes and walked over toward Lynn with her eyes seeking encouragement. He knew it was time to open the letter. She picked up the letter off the desk and hesitated, looking over to see what expression he might have on that handsome face.

Lynn's face never changed as he prepared to light his pipe and acted as if it was just another quiet Kansas evening. He sucked on the end of his pipe as he lit the match and turned the tobacco he packed carefully into glowing red embers. He blew out the smoke and shook the match to extinguish it. Inwardly, the excitement was building as much for him as it was for Emma, but he didn't show it.

"Well, go on Emma, open it," was all it took from his lips as he handed her the pocketknife he pulled from his overall pocket. She carefully opened the short blade that Lynn kept razor sharp. As she slid the knife carefully under the lip of the envelope at the corner, she held her breath and slit the envelope open. Closing the blade, she handed the knife back to her husband.

The feelings inside her were not new. When she read the letter from the adoption home about Philip five years earlier, it was one of the most exciting days of her life only matched by marrying Lynn and the birth of John Vernon. This time she was thinking of how she hoped she could have the little girl that she dreamed of being her own.

Emma slowly removed the letter she had been dying to read all day. She looked at the heading with the pictures of two beautiful babies, which reminded her of her own two baby boys. Emma took a seat in the straight-back chair close to Lynn and nervously read the letter out loud.

THE NURSERY
OF
The Willows Maternity Sanitarium
2929 MAIN STREET
KANSAS CITY, MISSOURI
March 21, 1925.

March 21, 1925

Mrs. L. V. Keller

Delia, Kansas

Dear Mrs. Keller:

We now have a girl baby that I would recommend for your home, and I am enclosing herewith the history of her parentage.

At the present time baby Marcia has brown eyes and hair. Her head and features are well formed and she is a bright healthy baby. Her Mother is a young girl from a good family and she is quite attractive in appearance. She is the daughter of a farmer, and the baby's paternal grandfather is also a farmer. Baby Marcia's mother was in our institution three months previous to confinement and during her stay here she always conducted herself in a ladylike manner, and was well liked by her associates and the nurses as well.

We have had the Wassermann blood test made on baby Marcia and her mother and both tests are negative, *therefore satisfactory. For these tests there is a charge of $10.00 in addition to the regular adoption fee of $21.00 making a total of $31.00 in all. The Wassermann test is a test for social diseases and baby Marcia's and her mother's blood are shown to be free of blood taints.*

Now, Mrs. Keller, I am going to make arrangements to hold this baby at your disposal until Tuesday or Wednesday, March 24th or 25th, and trust you can arrange to come here on one of those dates. If Mr. Keller cannot come with you it is satisfactory for you to come alone, as we can send the adoption paper there for him to sign after you return home with the baby. If you arrive here early in the morning, all arrangements can be made and completed so that you may return home the evening of that same day if you wish.

We recommend and feed our babies cows' milk. We shall be glad to give you the formula for preparing the baby's food. It could be well for you to bring with you a quart Thermos bottle and two Hygeia nursing bottles, or you may obtain them after you arrive here. We shall be glad to give you sufficient food to last the baby on your return trip home.

Hope to have the pleasure of meeting you personally on one of these dates stated above, I await your arrival.

Very truly yours,

Mrs. Nellie McEwen, Secy.

The Willows

A tear was running down Emma's cheek as she finished reading the letter to Lynn. He smiled and said, "Looks like you have a train to catch." Emma reread the dates for her arrival in Kansas City. Today was the 23rd and she had to be there by the 25th. She had a lot of work to do to get ready. A sigh of relief escaped and she gave Lynn a hug. With a little shriek of joy, she jumped up to get busy at all the tasks she needed to accomplish in the next 24 hours. Lynn just smiled that familiar grin as he watched his very excited wife and thought, "a little girl."

Chapter 50

As Emma, a quiet, loving, sweet-souled lady filled with joy in her heart, rode the east bound train to Kansas City to pick up her baby girl, she thought there must be a heart broken girl on her way back home alone.

A few weeks earlier a quiet, loving, sweet-souled young girl, wearing a blue and white gingham dress and saddle shoes, sat forlornly on a train heading southwest to her sister's home in Garnett, Kansas. It was just twelve days earlier that she gave birth to a precious baby girl. She was not even given one last chance to say goodbye to her beautiful baby girl, Marcia, one last hug, one last kiss on her forehead. Tears rolled down her cheek.

Leona said her goodbyes to Dottie, knowing she would never see her friend again. Nurse Jagger escorted Leona out of The Willows, and they descended the long steps to the street where a taxi was waiting to take Emma to Union Station. She was given a ticket and told which train she would be leaving on and the time. There was a quick embrace by Nurse Jagger and as the door to the taxi was closed, so too ended a chapter of Leona's life at The Willows. In many ways she felt so much older with all that she had gone through, but in actuality, she was still the quiet, shy young girl with a whole lifetime ahead of her. The only thing was, her heart was broken and she didn't know how she would be able to carry on without her baby girl.

At the train station, Leona sat sadly on the bench waiting for her train. She thought back to her last conversation with Mrs. Lowe that morning. Mrs. Lowe brought one last paper for Leona to sign dismissing her to go home. Leona already signed papers when she arrived at the Willows giving up any rights to her baby, which she dreaded ever doing. "Leona, you have been a very strong and well-behaved young lady during your stay," Mrs. Lowe said. "Now it is time for you to go back home and to start your new life. Your family has been notified that you will be on the train to your sister's today. They will meet you at the station."

Leona sat numb. She was leaving and without her daughter.

"You have been blessed to be able to start anew," Mrs. Lowe continued. "I want you to know the baby will have a wonderful Christian home and you have made the right decision. I want you to promise you will never look for the baby for her sake or interfere in her or the new parents' lives. It is what is best for the baby. Do you promise?"

Leona looked away from Mrs. Lowe. She stopped and thought for a moment and slowly nodded her head and barely above a whisper said, "Yes, I promise."

The train ride to Garnett, Kansas, seemed like it took an eternity but in actuality it took just a couple of hours even with all the stops between Kansas City and Garnett. Leona spent the entire time clutching her bag with her few belongings to her breast. She just stared out the window not seeing the landscape as it went by. It was the saddest day of her life, and she didn't know how she was going to carry on.

The train was rolling to a stop for what seemed like the hundredth time since Leona left Kansas City. This time the porter shouted, "Garnett!" Leona slowly rose and carried her bag to the front of the passenger car to exit. The porter held her hand as she carefully climbed down the steps. She no more than stepped onto the platform and she heard, "Ona!" She looked up and it was her sister, Iva. Oh how her sad heart leaped for joy in seeing a loving familiar face. Iva was alone and ran toward Leona. She reached her with open arms and the two sisters hugged and both were crying.

"Oh Ona, I am so happy to see you. Baby sister, I am so sorry for all you've gone through. I wish I'd been there for you. But you're home with me now. All will be okay."

Iva's words were very comforting but could not ease Leona's pain. Seeing a loved one after so much time, Leona felt for the first time in months that she wasn't alone. Deep in her soul, she knew a part of her heart was gone forever. Time would prove her wrong.

Chapter 51

August, 1991

It was the morning after my mother talked to her birth mother for the first time. I spent the night at the farm, and we stayed up talking and listening to the tape over and over. We called and talked to my sisters and shared the excitement. I never saw my mother happier. She and I sat at the breakfast table reflecting on the previous day's events. A tear rolled down her cheek when she once again shared Leona's words about having to give up "her baby Marcia" and promising never to look for her. So many of the questions that haunted my mother all these years were finally being answered. Her heart ached for Leona and the pain she went through. There was still so much to learn about each other.

For the first time, Mother began to realize why it had been so important for her to find her birth mother. She had wanted to find her for so long. She had felt guilty for having these feelings, needing to find her mother and to know why she gave her away. Mother knew in her heart how blessed she was to have such wonderful parents and family and should have been happy with that. But this desire from the moment she found out she was adopted had never gone away. After listening to Leona's story, she realized how much Leona had wanted her as well. They had needed to find each other.

Mother told Leona the night before how badly she had wanted to find her birth mother her whole life. Finding Leona was a dream come true. The fact Leona was made to promise to never look for "Marcia" helped heal the hurt my mother had felt. She never understood why her mother hadn't looked for her.

The night before I mentioned to Mother and Dad that I thought we should go to California and meet Leona. School didn't start for a few more weeks, and if Leona was up for us to come visit, I thought we should go. Wanda's heart beat wildly at the possibility to finally meet her mother face to face. "KelLee, nothing would make me happier."

My dad agreed and thought it was a great idea, but he couldn't leave the farm as he was extremely busy putting up prairie hay and getting fields ready for planting wheat. "You and your mom should go though," he said.

"When you call and talk to Leona tomorrow, ask her if it would be okay for us to come visit. She might not be ready though so don't be disappointed if she says not yet," I cautioned Mother.

Later that morning Randy arrived to start working on the house. Wanda pulled him aside and told him the news. He was the first person she actually got to tell about finding her birth mother. He was pretty shocked and gave her a hard time that she wouldn't want him for a nephew any more. She laughed and teased, "No way, at least not until you finish the remodel job and the deck."

Randy chuckled and said, "Well, hopefully by the time you get back from California, I'll be all finished with the remodeling and out of your hair. But who is going to make my lunches while you are gone, surely not Uncle Lee?"

Both laughed and she said, "I will be sure to leave an extra jar or two of mayonnaise since that's about all you eat with bread and a piece of meat. Think Lee can handle that."

That afternoon Mother called Leona and the conversation again flowed easily as if they had known each other for years and were best friends. They were both almost giddy with happiness as they shared back and forth, though they both admitted being a little tired from the lack of sleep. They talked about so many things—their husbands and families, their childhoods; their love of the outdoors and hunting and fishing; and their dislikes and likes. One point of conversation became a bit awkward when my mother asked, "Leona, I have been thinking about this all night. What would you like for me to call you?"

We were trained from an early age to never call my mother "Mom" but to call her "Mother." She really hated being called Mom for some reason and we never knew why. It was funny because she called her mother (my Grandma Emma) "Mom." She and Dad called Grandma Parr "Mom," too. In her mind, probably a very good reason not to be called "Mom." Whatever it was, we were told to only call her Mother. The funniest thing though was when she had her grandkids, they called her "Granny" and that was perfectly okay. Really? And we had to be formal, calling her "Mother."

So in this first conversation my mother and Leona discussed what to call each other. They decided my mother should call Leona "Mother Leona" rather than "Mom" or "Mother" out of respect for my Grandma Emma. We kids called her Grandma Leona.

It was very strange for Leona to call my mother "Wanda" since all these years in her mind she was Marcia. My mother told her it was okay if she wanted to call her either Marcia or Wanda, whichever was more comfortable. Their first few letters back and forth were written to or signed Marcia or Marcia/Wanda.

In one of Leona's letters a few months after getting to know all of us she wrote:

Dear Wanda,

I didn't call you Marcia because I met you as Wanda and I don't think the girls would want me to change your name. haha I know who you are and I love you by either name and so thankful KelLee got us together.

That was the last time Leona ever referred to my mother in a letter as Marcia.

Toward the end of the phone conversation that day, my mother asked Leona what her thoughts were to having visitors and if Leona was interested in meeting us in person. She told Leona that we would be open to flying out to California to meet her before I had to get back to teach school.

Leona was totally excited about the idea of meeting her daughter and grandson but her heart skipped a beat. The idea of meeting us was scary and the thought of "what if they don't like me" was running through her mind. The other thought was about the secret she had kept for so long. Very few people currently in her life knew her secret. Was she ready to divulge this secret in such a big way? She didn't hesitate too long and said, "I would love to meet you both. I have nothing going on so whenever works for you, I will be ready. The closest airport is in Klamath Falls, Oregon. I can meet you there and pick you up."

"That sounds great. We will check on reservations and let you know," Mother answered back not giving Leona a chance to change her mind.

We made our reservations for the next week. Mother was on pins and needles all week packing and trying to prepare herself to meet Leona. She had spent countless hours on the phone telling her family and friends about finding Mother Leona. She could hardly contain herself, acting like a young schoolgirl. The first person she called to tell was her best friend, Genevieve Matyak. She knew Genevieve would give her good advice and be excited for her.

Genevieve probably knew my mother better than anyone. They confided in each other about everything. The two were best friends ever since they were freshmen in high school. When they finished school, they moved to Topeka to find jobs and roomed together. The two even dated brothers, Paul and Frank Matyak. Genevieve eventually married Paul, but my mother and Frank just remained friends. When Mother returned with her brother from California years earlier, Genevieve told her that Frank was home from the military and asked about her. My mother told Genevieve that she wasn't interested in dating Frank. She had talked to a fortune teller and was told she was marrying a handsome farmer. Mother knew exactly who she meant. It was Leroy Parr. My mother also told Genevieve about the fortune teller's promise that one day she would find her birth mother.

The best friends and their husbands were lifelong friends. Coincidentally, Paul and Genevieve lived and raised their family in my Great-grandma Celestia Keller's old home. Mother told us she always thought of her childhood memories with Grandma Celestia every time she visited Genevieve. There were very few days that went by that my mother and Genevieve didn't talk on the phone for hours, usually late at night after their hubbies had gone to bed. So Genevieve was over the moon when Mother gave her the news about finding Leona.

Mother's news was an even bigger surprise than the day Genevieve called to tell her that she was pregnant at the age of 45 with her sixth child and scared to death. Genevieve's youngest was already thirteen. Mother was Genevieve's rock through this time. Nothing expressed more their true friendship than the day the local TV station news anchor, Betty Lou Pardu, traveled 30 miles to the farm and knocked on the Parr front door with a dozen red roses to surprise my mother. She told Mother she had been nominated by Genevieve and won their Valentine's Day Best Friend contest.

Genevieve, with her youngest daughter Monica's help, submitted an entry to the station writing about their friendship and that my mother's birthday was Valentine's Day. Her entry was chosen from the hundreds of entries. Mother was overwhelmed with emotion by her friend's love. The two won a trip to Topeka to dine at Olive Garden, which was a big deal in those days. A white limousine picked the two up at Genevieve's house in Delia along with Genevieve's daughters, who joined them for a day of pampering.

There was no one who truly understood and appreciated my mother's emotions any better than her best friend, Genevieve. She was aware of the deep loss my mother felt in being given up for adoption and not knowing her birth mother. She also knew how finding Leona filled the void in her heart. Genevieve asked Mother, "Do you remember what you told me when you returned home from California and you'd seen that fortune teller?"

"Yes, I sure do. I've thought about that a lot."

"Amazing after all these years, the fortune teller's promise to find your birth mother came true."

"Sure took long enough," my mother chuckled.

The best friends laughed and wept together with joy.

Chapter 52

Just a few days after our first conversations with Leona, my mother and I left from Kansas City and flew to Sacramento where we caught a little commuter flight for Klamath Falls and our five day visit. Sixty-six years earlier, Leona boarded a train that took her away from her daughter. On this beautiful summer day, Mother and I boarded a plane that would reunite them. The commuter plane held about twenty people with single passenger seats on each side of the plane. This was the smallest plane either of us had ever flown in before. With my six-foot-two frame, I had to practically double over to get to my seat. It was a little nerve racking, but it was worth it to meet Leona.

The pilot welcomed us then told us to expect a lot of turbulence. It was going to be a bumpy flight. Between Mother's anxiety about meeting Leona and our trepidation about the small plane, it seemed turbulence, whether real or emotional, would define the day.

Mother tried to smile and act like all was okay. The closer we got to Leona, the more apprehensive she became. "What if Leona is disappointed when she sees me" she asked repeatedly, each time as if it were the first. We hadn't had time to exchange photos so neither had any idea what the other looked like. I encouraged her to relax and not to worry because Leona would think she was wonderful. At that moment, my fear was not would Leona and my mother like each other, but would our flight be bumpy. I was afraid it was not going to be the "Fly the Friendly Skies" experience as advertised on TV.

MY LITTLE VALENTINE

Anyone who knew my mother well would have known a bumpy flight would not have been a good thing. Saying my mother had a queasy stomach was an understatement. Roller coaster—not an option! We all knew on family car trips to be prepared for carsickness. Mother never could ride in the back seat without getting sick. (Maybe this started back during Leona's first car ride!) Though amazingly on trips with their friends the Millers and Dodges, the three men sat up front and the three women all sat in the back seat. We always figured amusingly that maybe her not getting carsick with them had to do with the extreme compactness and lack of movement.

Jane, Jan and I never understood the daredevil in our mother, who always wanted to try new things even when she knew it was likely going to make her sick. She enjoyed flying, went up in a helicopter on a dare, and loved riding the ski lifts in the Colorado mountains in the summer. One of her biggest wishes was to ride in a hot air balloon. She never got to go up in the hot air balloon even though Genevieve's son had it lined up to take her and her cousin Arlene when Mother was 78 years old, but windy weather prohibited it from happening. Thinking back, I am surprised that Mother's answer to my question "what is the one thing she would want" wasn't "ride in a hot air balloon" instead of "paint the old red barn."

My niece EJ got to experience both the daredevil and queasy side of "Granny" when she and my sisters took Mother to Hawaii on her 80th birthday, another of her life-long dreams. While on the beach one day, they saw a sign for parasailing over the ocean. Mother was adamant she wanted to go. The family joke is that EJ drew the short straw. In actuality, she was happy to honor her grandmother's wish and accompanied her on the exciting ride, sailing over the ocean to the amazement of my sisters and all the others watching. Folks in their tour group that had been afraid to go said, "If at 80 Granny Wanda can parasail, so can we."

The grandmother and granddaughter made a wonderful lifelong memory that day, but the adventure didn't come without a price. As EJ put it with a chuckle, "Thankfully we were out over the ocean."

So as the two of us headed north toward Klamath Falls in what Mother later referred to as "the crop duster," we bounced up and down several times between impossibly short smooth periods. Mother clutched her "barf" bag. Thankfully our prayers were answered and the bag remained in its original condition. The flight seemed much longer than the announced time, but we made it safely and were both happy when those tiny tires hit the runway. Mother was a little green around the gills after we landed, but that quickly went away with the happy thoughts of finally meeting her birth mother.

The commuter taxied to the tiny terminal. The ground crew quickly pushed the air stairs around to the side of the plane for us to disembark. No airbridge at Klamath Regional Airport. Looking through the little plane window that framed the terminal building, Wanda thought to herself, "My mother is just feet away!"

Wanda was a 66 year old, beautiful silver-haired, full-figured to slightly overweight, dignified lady with bum knees. Her bad knees were a result of playing catcher on a softball team as a young woman, driving the tractor and combine for years, and working hard all her life. The doctors said she needed knee replacement surgery but that would come much later in life. Going down stairs was a bit of a challenge but even with her aches and pains, she was always a pretty good trooper and not much slowed her down. The flight attendant grabbed her arm and helped Mother as she carefully climbed down the air stairs to the tarmac. I was right behind her. At the bottom of the steps we looked at each other and smiled. "Well, are you ready for this?" I asked.

"As ready as I'll ever be."

My mother took my arm and we grabbed our carry-on bags. We followed the others to the entrance to the terminal. Airport travel was so much easier then. The airport security, or lack thereof, was a breeze. We passed through the terminal door and started looking around at all the people congregated just waiting for their loved ones.

Since we hadn't had time to exchange photos, we had no idea what Leona looked like. At the very same time, we both spotted a frail, thin woman with reddish brown hair, glasses and a huge smile. She was wearing a white short-sleeve blouse with blue slacks, just like she described so we could identify her. Mother told Leona she would be wearing a red blouse and white pants. She figured that would stand out in a crowd. I advised Leona to just look for the tall guy next to the lady in red.

Leona gently waved at us and Mother squeezed my arm. We waved back and headed toward her. Reaching this sweetest looking little lady, my mother said, "You must be Leona. I am your Marcia. You have no idea how happy I am to meet you."

Leona just smiled and said, "I am so happy to meet you, honey."

My mother and Leona hugged and cried tears of happiness and couldn't really say anything. I teared up just watching the two embrace. They didn't want to let go but eventually Mother said, "I have dreamed of meeting you my whole life. I was afraid I would never find you."

"I never thought this would happen either and still can't believe it," Leona said.

"This is my son KelLee, your grandson," Mother said. "We wouldn't have found each other if it wasn't for him."

"It is so nice to meet you. I can't thank you enough for finding me." And she gave me a huge hug.

Talk about an Oprah moment. I was expecting Oprah and her crew to jump out at any moment with cameras rolling. After our hug, they hugged again. No one could have wiped the smiles off their faces. All the passengers' luggage was delivered in the terminal, and we got our bags and Leona said, "Let's head home. We have a lot of catching up to do."

It was amazing how young and spry she was at 83 years of age. She was only about 5'5" and 110 pounds soaking wet. It was obvious she was quite nervous but her smile was huge and the sparkle in her eyes helped me know this was a very special moment for her as well.

Leona's car was meticulously clean and reminded me how Mother always kept our cars clean even with living out on the country roads. We loaded our luggage in the trunk and climbed in. Leona said she hoped we didn't mind her driving. That made me a little nervous, especially fresh off the "crop duster." I took the backseat making sure Mother was sitting up front. There was no threat of us exceeding the speed limit on the ride to her house, but my fears were for naught, Leona was an excellent driver. The countryside was beautiful, and I could see why she was so in love with this area. She told us that it was about 18 miles to her house in Dorris. There were mountains off to the west and we drove through a long valley with lots of pastures and fields and not too many houses.

The conversation during the ride just flowed. You would have thought we had known each other all our lives. We shared about our bumpy flight and we were glad Mother didn't get airsick. Leona told us that she would sometimes get carsick, riding in the back seat. She said, "I also love to go fishing out on the ocean, but I usually end up getting seasick. It never stopped me from wanting to go." I smiled.

Leona told a little about her day and getting ready for our arrival. We laughed about how wild this was to finally meet after all these years. Leona commented on my mother's beautiful silver hair and how pretty she was. Mother blushed and I could tell that meant the world to her. Leona went on to tell us, "I dye my hair cause when it started to turn white, my husband, Russell, told me

I was too young to be an old gray-haired woman. So I started dying it and never stopped." Laughing with her cute little chuckle she went on to say, "But something went way wrong this time. Normally it is light brown but it turned out this reddish color and I hate it. I need a perm too but didn't have time to get one. And here you was coming to meet me. I figured you would see this old, scraggly red-headed woman and get back on that plane."

We laughed and Mother said, "It looks just fine. You are just as pretty as I always imagined and I am so glad to get to know you. I would be happy to give you a perm while I am here if you would like."

"Oh that's too much trouble."

"No, it will be fun. I would love to do that for you." About the third day of our visit the house was filled with the strong odor from the permanent. They shared a special mother/daughter experience for the first time. So many of these moments they had missed.

Arriving at her house, we pulled up to a separate small garage next to a cute little brick house. The front was filled with all kinds of flowers and there was a porch with chairs that looked like would be a perfect spot to spend a quiet evening, watching the sun go down. My mother commented on Leona's beautiful flowers and how she loved planting and taking care of her flowers on the farm. We got our luggage out of the car, and noticed all the deer and elk antlers hanging up near the rafters on the garage walls. Mother said, "It looks like Russell liked to hunt."

Leona laughed and said, "Well, he sure did but half of those are from ones I shot. We both loved to hunt and loved to fish, too."

I was reading my mother's mind. It was a well-known fact that my mother loved to hunt and fish as a young girl growing up. She still fished at the farm ponds around the house. Mother would always rather be outdoors playing ball or hunting and fishing with the boys. Her sisters Naomi and Geneva both would rather be in the house playing with their dolls and helping their mom with cooking and canning. We were starting to learn just how much my mother and Leona had in common. "Oh, I have always loved to hunt and fish," Mother said. "Never shot any elk but shot plenty of white-tailed deer when I was young. I never hunted much after getting married. Lee wasn't much of a hunter."

We carried our bags up to the porch and Leona unlocked the front door. She welcomed us into her lovely home. It was spotless and everything in its place. Another thing the two had in common. The first thing we noticed was the beautiful white brick fireplace that majestically filled the entire wall. It had a lovely wooden mantel. Hanging above the mantel was a vibrant landscape painting of geese flying over a coastal scene. There were just a few photos and we asked about them. Leona said they were of her niece Darlene, nephew Orville and their families. The rest of the mantel was filled with large seashells Leona had picked up at the ocean and knickknacks, much like what my mother loved to display.

She showed us to our rooms to drop off our luggage and then the rest of the house. One of the first things Leona told us upon getting settled in was that she hadn't told anybody but her brother Bud and niece Lola about us or that we were coming to visit. She said she would like for us to meet Bud, but she hadn't gotten up the courage to tell Orville and Darlene.

Leona told us about her brother Louis and how there was no one she was closer to than him. He had been her rock her whole life. She so wished he were still alive to meet us. Louis had passed on from a heart attack so long ago in 1966. Louis' wife, Ruby, lived in a nearby town. Leona said, "I was so close to Louis, and Ruby is like a sister to me. But I haven't ever told her about you. I would like for you to meet her and for her to get to know you, if that's okay?"

"We would love to meet anyone you would like," Mother said.

Leona told us about a nosy neighbor, Alma, across the street she was friends with for years. Another neighbor next door named Ray Allen was really nice to her and helped her when she needed anything. Of course they knew nothing about us, and she wasn't quite ready to let them know she had a whole new family and a past secret. Alma would want to know who was visiting. Leona asked, "Would you mind if for now we just said we were friends if either of them stop by? I've never told a soul other than Russell that I had a baby, and I really don't know if I am ready to explain all that yet."

We smiled and said we certainly understood and definitely didn't want to make things uncomfortable for her. We said to just tell people that we were friends from back home in Kansas, which was true. She thanked us and said, "I made some banana bread if you are hungry. I should get to fixin' us some supper. You must be starved."

Years later Grandma Leona wrote to Mother:

Alma stopped by and was braggin' on her grandchildren. I just smiled. I didn't tell Alma I had a grandson and two granddaughters and two great grandchildren. Ha, ha. I am proud of all of you.

Chapter 53

The stay with Leona was great fun, and we learned so much about her life. She told us about Russell and that he had died of a heart attack in 1977. It was obvious from the tone in her voice she truly loved and missed him.

We learned more about Leona's life with Russell as they worked together on Orman Road construction near Crater Lake in Oregon. It was nice with Louis being there, too. It was a hard life. They lived in a tent alongside the roads they were building. She was one of the few women on the work crew. "It could get really cold in the winters," Leona said. "But we loved being able to work outside, and it was so beautiful at Crater Lake. Once we had enough money, we got us one of those silver Airstream trailers, and it made living conditions so much better. We would all camp in the same campground with our trailer houses. We had a beautiful German shepherd dog that everyone in the camp loved."

Leona once wrote to Mother:

> *One of our old construction buddies passed away October 27th. Our old friends, men especially, are about all gone. Guess women are tougher than men. Ha ha. Maybe we don't work as hard as they do. Ha ha.*

Leona asked if we would like to go up to Crater Lake. We of course jumped at the chance. She asked me if I would mind driving because she didn't like driving in the mountains anymore, and I was glad to drive. The whole day was a beautiful adventure.

We were amazed at the winding, steep roads and envisioned how difficult a way of life it was for Leona, Russell, and Louis when they were helping carve the roads.

Crater Lake was some of the most beautiful scenery I had ever seen. No wonder Leona loved it so much. It was perfectly clear and sunny, and Leona said we couldn't have hit a nicer day. At the gift shop at the top of the mountain, Leona asked if she could buy us a souvenir. She bought a Crater Lake thimble for Mother's thimble collection and a Crater Lake bell with a bear for me. What a great day it was!

On our way back home, Leona said we would go by and visit Ruby. She had called Ruby to tell her she was coming and bringing visitors but didn't say who. When we got there, Ruby invited us to come in and sit down. She was pretty feeble and couldn't stand very well. Mother and Leona sat on the couch on either side of Ruby. Leona introduced us to her lovely sister-in-law. Leona said, "Well Ruby, this is my daughter Wanda and my grandson KelLee. I wanted you to meet them."

Ruby had a little stunned look on her face and then smiled and looked at Leona and said, "But I thought you had a boy." And we all had a good laugh.

Come to find out Ruby said she had heard rumors back when she and Louis first got married. Some folk were talking at some family get-together that Leona had a baby but Louis never talked about it. She said, "It was none of my business and I just adored Leona. I just felt bad for her if it was true."

Ruby was a delight and we had a wonderful chat and she was so happy for Leona.

The next day, Leona took us to Klamath Falls to show us the town and wanted us to see where she and Russell had lived. Leona shared how they decided to move to Klamath Falls when they found out they were going to have Darlene and Orville to raise. Russell found a construction job in town and they bought the first house they ever owned. "I just loved this house," Leona shared. "It was the first time I had my own kitchen and indoor bathroom."

She went on to tell us, "When Orville reached high school, he started getting into some trouble and not doing well in school. Russell kept saying Orville needed to be working to stay out of trouble. One day Russell came home and announced that, unbeknownst to me, he had purchased a rundown little farm outside of Dorris, California. The house was just a little shack with no running water or indoor plumbing."

"I was spitting mad he bought that place without even talking to me," Leona added. "I cried having to give up my nice house for this old scrub brush farmstead. But in the long run, Russell was right and it kept Orville out of trouble. We had to work extremely hard to make ends meet, but we turned the little farm into a home and livelihood."

On our final day trip, Leona had me drive out to visit the old farmstead, and we could tell it must have taken a tremendous amount of work keeping it going. The terrain was rough and pretty barren. A far cry from the rich Kansas soil we were used to seeing. In 1969 Russell decided it was time for them to move back into town. They sold the farm and bought the house she was currently living in.

Leona wrote in one of her letters to Mother:

> *Thank God we got our place sold before Russell passed away and we did have from '69 to '77 to go places and enjoy ourselves and little hunting and fishing too.*

Leona told us it was pretty lonely with Russell gone, but she kept busy with her garden. She was happy that Orville and his wife, Betty, lived nearby. They were good to her and checked on her often. Leona loved sharing stories of how Orville enjoyed the local chariot racing, where teams of horses raced pulling two-wheeled chariots. When we told my dad later, he thought this sounded right up his alley. Orville and his boys kept her firewood box full, and they stopped by often for some of her pie. Leona loved to cook as long as she had people to feed. Pretty much the same way my mother was about cooking. They both were excellent cooks.

One of Leona's letters summed it up:

Betty came by about noon yesterday for pie and today Orville came in for lunch. Then a friend stopped by and ate a piece of pie so don't have much left now. Time to cook again. I love to cook and glad to have them.

On the other hand, Darlene lived about 260 miles away on a ranch in Oregon with her husband, Joe. Joe was ill with multiple sclerosis. Darlene and her son, Geren, ran the ranch now and had a lot of cattle. Geren was in his 20s and doing a good job of keeping things going since his papa was so ill. Leona missed getting to see them more often.

Leona wrote to Mother about driving:

Alma won't even drive to Klamath Falls. Goes with me if she wants. And it don't take me too long to go over to Ruby's. Wish Darlene didn't live quite so far away. 260 miles one way, but I don't really mind it, when I make up my mind I just go.

A couple of days into our visit, Leona invited her brother, Bud, and his wife, Millie, to the house to meet us. They were just as sweet to us as could be. Millie was a talker and she was just totally amazed to find out about us. We discovered Bud never told Millie that Leona had a baby. Millie laughed, "Bud never shared that little bit of trivia with me."

Bud chimed in defensively, "It wasn't none of your business and if Leona had wanted to tell you, she would've." I guess little Bud could keep a secret after all.

Millie told me privately how interesting it was looking back now because some things were starting to make sense. "You know Leona would never want to hold or pick up any of the new babies when they were born into the family. She would say she would drop and break them. It wasn't until they were old enough to walk that she would start to pay any attention to the kids."

Later that evening after Bud and Millie left, I asked Leona about what Millie had said regarding her and babies. Leona had a sad look on her face and shared, "It was because I could never hold a baby without thinking of my baby Marcia and those few days she was with me at the home in Kansas City. It was just too hard."

During a second trip the next year to visit Grandma Leona, we went to Bud and Millie's house. They were foster parents as well as having three daughters of their own. They mostly took in babies and very small children until adoptive parents were found for them.

Millie had tons of baby clothes, dolls, and children's toys around their house to accommodate the foster kids. She had lots of garage sales to get rid of all the extra stuff she accumulated. Millie's daughter was having a garage sale the day we went to visit. Leona and Mother had fun looking at all the "stuff" that was out for sale. The two were looking at the baby clothes and toys and Leona said to Mother, "I never got to buy you any of these nice baby things."

She picked up a beautiful baby-size doll with a cute little hand-crocheted sweater and hat. She looked at Mother and said, "Every birthday or Christmas I wondered if you were given a doll to play with. I always wanted to buy you a doll. Would it be okay if I bought this doll for you?"

Mother put her arm around Leona's shoulder, took the doll in her other arm, and with tears in her eyes said, "I would love to have this doll from you." From that time on, the cute little doll with the crocheted sweater and hat Leona bought sat proudly on my mother's bed.

Chapter 54

During that first visit to Dorris, California, there were lots of similarities found that Leona and Wanda shared, and it was more than just coincidence. Of course there was the love for hunting and fishing. The two also discovered they shared a trait they wished they didn't. Leona couldn't carry a tune if her life depended on it. Wanda was exactly the same way and hated not being able to sing. Wanda told Leona the story of how when she was a little girl she just loved to sing. One year the children in her one-room schoolhouse were preparing for a Christmas singing program. Her teacher and cousin, Christina Bowers, stopped in the middle of practice and singled out Wanda telling her to not sing so loudly because she was off pitch. She was terribly embarrassed. She told Leona she didn't sing for years. In church she would just mouth the words.

When Wanda was 50 years old, she went to the local voice and piano teacher, Mary Jane Berkey, and asked if Mary Jane would give her singing lessons. She gave piano lessons to most every kid in town and many teenagers wanted her as their vocal coach to be prepared to sing in the high school choir. Mary Jane told Wanda she would be happy to give her voice lessons. After about three lessons, she suggested Wanda try piano lessons.

So both Leona and Wanda loved music but could only enjoy listening. Leona brought down an antique 1910 Edison Horn Cylinder phonograph from the attic. It was in amazing condition with its red, flower-shaped horn and brown wooden box. There were 20 or 30 of the cardboard cylinders with the words Edison

Gold Mould Recording scrolled across the front in red and brown ink. Alma, Leona's neighbor, happened to stop by to visit and joined in listening to the wonderful old tunes like "The Glowworm," "Meet Me in St. Louis," "Silent Night," and "The Star Spangled Banner" just to name a few. What a wonderful time it was.

One other not so good thing that Leona and Wanda had in common was high blood pressure. Leona stopped at lunch to take her one and only daily pill. She was extremely healthy for 83 years old, but she had had high blood pressure almost her entire adult life. Wanda told her she had high blood pressure, too. Her doctor gave her several medicines to try but nothing really worked well. One medicine helped lower her blood pressure but gave her a bad lingering cough. Leona told her the name of the medicine she took and for years it had worked really well for her. It was a new name for Wanda. When she got back to Kansas, she asked her doctor. He said she could sure give it a try. It was one she hadn't tried before. From the moment Wanda started taking the medicine, she never had another issue with high blood pressure.

One day while visiting, Leona shared more about Orville's children. He had two boys, Russell and Louis, named after their great uncles. Leona told us that Louis was especially close to her, and he came to visit her quite often even now that he was grown and out of school. She said that it just so happened his birthday was February 14.

When Louis was very little, Leona started making him a birthday cake on his birthday. He was the only one of the great nieces and nephews she would make a birthday cake. Leona said, "I always said it was because I felt sorry for him because he got cheated, having his birthday on a holiday. I knew how that felt since my birthday was on December 29 and so close to Christmas. My birthday often just got celebrated when we all got together for Christmas. So I baked and decorated a cake for Louis. But in all honesty, every time I made that birthday cake, it was also for my little Valentine Marcia. I would hope someone made a cake for her."

That first visit went way too fast and it was time to head back to Kansas. It was totally amazing how well Wanda and Leona got along. How similar they were in many ways with mannerisms and even how they talked. They realized they both were very strong-willed women and in their own words "hard headed." Leona joked to Wanda, "We probably would have had a rough time of it when you was growing up because we would have butted heads and neither given in."

It was sad to say goodbye but both mother and daughter knew they had just started a new chapter in their lives. Before leaving to go back home, Wanda placed a little box on Leona's dresser. It was a gift that signified how much it meant to her to find Leona.

Chapter 55

Over the next few weeks, Leona and Wanda wrote many letters and called and talked on the phone almost daily. They had so many years to catch up on.

Leona's first letter to Wanda after that first visit read:

Sunday, 4:30 P.M. Aug. 4, 1991

Dear Marcia,

I went into my bedroom for something and I saw a little box over by my cards. I picked it up and looked inside and what did I see, this little gold heart that says "Together we are complete." Of course I had to cry. To think how long it has took us to get together. So thankful we finally did.

Oh, I called Lola today and told her about your visit. I also talked to Darlene but didn't tell her about us yet. She has all she can take right now with her husband Joe being ill. I told her we went and saw Ruby. I haven't seen Betty and Orville yet to tell them about you.

Ray Allen couldn't figure out why just friends would make that trip out here. Ha. I said, "Well, they like me."

I hope you had a good trip home and wasn't too tired. Oh Jane called. She thought you would still be here. She sounds a lot like you and I know I will like her. Hope to hear from you soon.

My love to you all,

I love you.

Mother

That sounds so odd. I have been Aunt Leona for so long but never forgot you. Didn't think I would ever get to say it.

Wanda wrote her back in her next letter:

Dear Mother Leona,

I want you to know how wonderful it was to see you and finally meet you after all these years. It was a dream and prayers that came true. I told my best friend Genevieve that I knew you as soon as we walked in the door and saw you standing there smiling. It was such a relief to find that you are just a down to earth country girl at heart and not sitting in a big mansion on the top of a hill somewhere. haha

KelLee and I both think you are great and we really enjoyed our week with you. We both enjoyed seeing and hearing the old phonograph, as well as I am sure Alma did too. haha

Wanda's letter finished:

We are looking forward to your visit in October. Thanks again for everything. It surely was nice visiting you and meeting Dale and Ruby. I still laugh when I remember Ruby's face and her saying, "but I thought you had a boy." Ha

I will write again soon or call you and you do the same.

My love,

Marcia

There wasn't a week when letters weren't exchanged. They both loved to send newspaper clippings and funny stories they read. Another thing they had in common. They truly became close and developed a deep love for one another. So appreciative that they had found each other.

Chapter 56

Grandma Leona visited Kansas in October. She had told us that she never ever planned to come back to Kansas because she hated to fly. Her niece, Lola, in Garnett was always begging her to come visit but every time she had politely declined.

When we were visiting Leona for the first time, my mother asked Leona if she would come back to Kansas to visit. Mother told her she would love for Leona to meet the rest of the family. "Jane, Jan and her family would come home to meet you," she said. "They are so excited to get to know you."

My mother offered to buy Leona a plane ticket and pick her up in Kansas City and take her to Garnett to see her niece as well. Leona promised to think about it.

Leona's cousin, Alfred, and his wife, Helen, lived in Tulsa, Oklahoma. They, too, had invited Leona to visit for years. About the same time Mother asked Leona to come to the farm and meet the family, Alfred contacted Leona and asked her again to come see them. He offered to pick her up at the airport in Tulsa and take her to Kansas to visit Lola. Lola could take her to Kansas City to fly home.

This was all it took. Flying on a plane truly wasn't something Grandma Leona wanted to do, but she couldn't pass up the chance to see her family and come meet her son-in-law, granddaughters and great-grandchildren. Leona booked a flight to leave on October 8 to Tulsa, Oklahoma, and would stay four weeks leaving November 5 from Kansas City.

She wrote Wanda:

> *I called and talked to Helen last night to see if this was okay, if it wasn't I could get my money back. Helen said, Oh no, we will meet you. I got a ticket for four weeks. Figure I could come up there about October 29 or a little earlier if not a bother.*

Alfred and Helen met her at the airport and spent a few days visiting in Tulsa. Leona never mentioned anything about my mother or that she was going to visit her daughter and family after staying with Lola. She wasn't quite ready to share her secret. Though she was very proud of her long lost daughter, Leona just wasn't able to talk about her past, worrying what people would think of her.

It took Leona some time to feel comfortable telling her loved ones about her secret. Leona shared with Mother:

> *I did write to Claude Hendrickson and told him not to tell everyone. Haven't had time to hear from him yet. I thanked him for telling KelLee where I was. Give me time and I will tell Orville. First time I see Darlene, I will tell her and take pictures over for her to see.*

Leona finally told Orville and Darlene about Mother in April of 1992, over eight months after reuniting. She was so scared to tell them about her long-kept secret and what they would think. But she knew she had to tell them and wanted them to meet her daughter and new family members. Their reactions were totally different. Leona explained in a letter:

> *I am so glad I told Darlene about us. She was happy for us. I told her you were coming back to visit this summer and she said she would sure come over, even if for just one night.*

Orville's reaction was quite different. He was upset at the news and the long-kept secret. He got mad and stormed out. It took him a while to adjust to the idea of new family members and Leona having kept this secret. Leona continued in her letter:

> Orville talked to me yesterday and he said he sure wanted to see you folks. Said he was sorry the way he acted but he was just jealous of me as I had always been his mother but he feels better about it now. Guess he found out I wasn't perfect. haha

On July 20, 1992, Leona wrote after Mother and Jane's visit that summer:

> Orville came in for lunch today. He is sure proud of <u>both</u> of you. He said I should tell everyone who you are. I will, then if people don't like me, I don't care for I have <u>you</u>.

After visiting Alfred and Helen, the three drove to Garnett. They stopped along the way in Havana to see their parents' and grandparents' graves. They drove down the old gravel road Leona walked to town to the dance so many years ago. Memories came rushing back. Their old farmstead was hard to find as it was grown up in cedar and hedge trees. They stopped where Leona was pretty sure the old house once stood and the only remnants of the farm they found were the shambles of the old barn. It tugged at Leona's heart as she thought of the good and bad times she'd spent here on Papa and Mama's farm.

Leona was happy to be in Garnett and to see Lola. It was far too long since she last saw her oldest niece. She hugged and thanked Lola for her advice to write me back. Leona admitted she wasn't sure she would have if Lola hadn't been so encouraging and understanding. Leona loved telling Lola all about Mother and our visit. There were so few she felt comfortable sharing with and being able to express her joy. She showed Lola her gold heart necklace and said she never took it off.

It was late October when Grandma Leona made it to the farm to see us after her visit with Lola. Mother and Dad went to Garnett to meet the new cousins and to pick up Leona. She had a little over a week to spend at the farm. Jane flew in from Florida and Jan, her husband, Louie, and kids, Bo and EJ, drove up from Texas.

As daunting as it was for Grandma Leona to come meet a bunch of new people, at least she knew Mother and me and talked to Dad, Jane and Jan on the phone many times. I think the scariest part for her was meeting Mother's brothers and sisters and family and how they would react. No need for worry. The visit was fantastic and Leona truly became a part of our family that visit. All of the Keller family opened their arms to Leona and welcomed her into the clan and thanked her for bringing Wanda to the family.

Chapter 57

From 1991 until Leona's passing in 2004, Wanda and Leona wrote at least weekly as well as talked on the phone. They took advantage of the huge miracle of finding each other and caught up on all the years they missed. Wanda kept every single letter, paper article clipping and card she received from her mother, filling a huge box over the years. The two shared some very intimate moments, often writing about how difficult it had been for Leona to give "Marcia" up for adoption and for Wanda to not know who her mother was. Leona shared how she worried not knowing if her baby was taken care of properly and was happy.

Wanda's sister, Geneva, loved to write and one of her endeavors was to write a book about the Keller family. It was called *"Precious Keller" Memories*. Geneva did a lot of research about the family history and interviewed family members asking each to share a favorite family memory. It was an amazing tribute to Grandpa and Grandma Keller and all the wonderful times each family member remembered.

For Christmas 1993, Wanda gave one of her sister's books to Leona and wrote on the inside cover:

To Mother Leona,

Merry Christmas

I'm sending you this book with my love, so you will better understand the loving family I was brought up in. I hope you enjoy it and never have any more doubt in your heart that you did the best thing for me by giving me up for adoption.

My love,

Marcia-Wanda

That first year brought many firsts for Leona and Wanda. The joy they shared in their first Christmas, Valentine's Day, and Mother's Day as mother and daughter. They expressed their appreciation over and over in their letters as each special event passed.

The first Christmas:

December 3, 1991

Now don't send me anything for xmas. My visit with you folks and finding you was best xmas anyone would want. Wish I lived closer to all of you, no luck. I can still come and see you and you all can come and see me.

Wanda's "first" birthday:

February 17, 1992

Dear Wanda and Lee,

I'll write a few lines while I am waiting for Betty to come. She is going to put a permanent in my hair. I haven't had one since you gave me one so you know it needs it. Wish it was you giving it to me.

I got your Valentine Thursday. Made me cry but it was happy tears. I had Louis's birthday dinner Saturday. I baked a heart shaped cake two layers. It was Betty

Crocker Cherry Cake Mix. I put red icing on it, then maraschino cherries around on top and give it to him to take home. It was nice making it for you too this time because I know you now.

Leona gave Wanda for her birthday a subscription to *Country Woman* magazine. She wrote:

Have you got that Country Woman yet? I had a card from them thanking me for sending you one. So if you don't get it let me know and I'll write to them. I told them I would like for it to be there for your birthday. Thought you might enjoy since we are both country gals. haha

For their first Mother's Day Leona wrote:

May 10, 1992

I just want to tell you this is the best Mother's Day I have ever had. Got your card and Jane and Janice's Friday. Then talked to you today. I didn't have to worry about you and where you were for you folks found me and that makes me very happy.

Wish you could have walked into my life a lot sooner. I sure love you and will enjoy what years I have with you. I am a tough old bird and have a lot of years left. HA I hope!

Chapter 58

One of the more delicate topics was to learn more detail about Mother's birth father. Leona wasn't very open talking about him at first. The more comfortable she and my mother became, the more Leona opened up and shared about the story of "the most handsome man I had ever seen when I went dancing" and hiding her good dress in the rafters of the outhouse to sneak out all those years ago.

We learned how she was so scared to tell anyone when she figured out she was pregnant and Louis took her to Nick's dad's farm to confront him. That's when they got to the farm and found out Nick had just recently gotten married after getting another girl pregnant. Leona laughed and said painfully, "He was what we called a real 'rounder' back in that day."

Leona wrote in a letter to Wanda:

> "Nick" Virgle Belt lived south of Elk City and west. I don't think too far from Sedan, Kansas and probably in Chautauqua County. I think his dad's name was Archie, they had a farm. That's been a long time ago and I was there only once, so don't remember to well.

So we learned that Nick lived on a farm northeast of Sedan, Kansas. His dad was a pretty wealthy farmer. On one of my visits to see Grandma Leona, I asked her if she knew what had happened to Nick. She had a little sad look in her eyes and said, "No, I don't know what has happened to him. I never saw him again after that trip to his dad's farm."

My mother never talked about finding her birth father that I remember. She really only wanted to find Leona. Part of that came from the fact Mother knew Leona May Hendrickson was her birth mother's name from some of the adoption records but there was no name or much information about her birth father. The only information on her father was a document from The Willow's announcing baby Marcia's birth and the parents' heritage. It read:

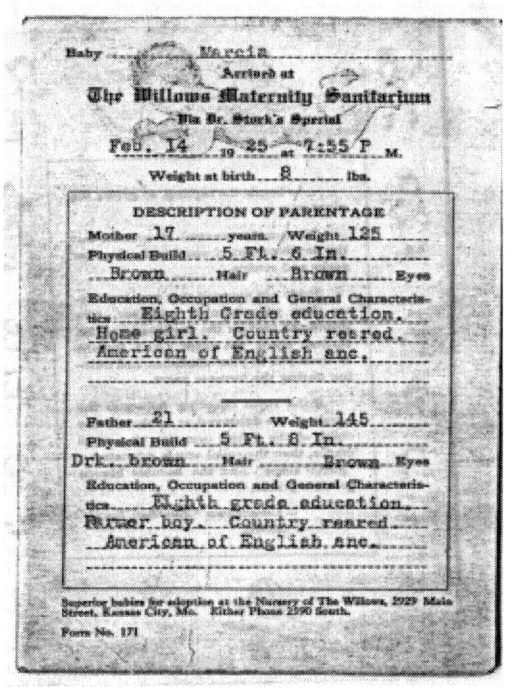

```
Baby _____Marcia_____
                    Arrived at
        The Willows Maternity Sanitarium
              Via Dr. Stork's Special
        Feb. 14____ 19 25 at 7:55 P M.
              Weight at birth ___8___ lbs.

        DESCRIPTION OF PARENTAGE
    Mother  17    years.  Weight 125
    Physical Build   5 Ft. 6 In.
    Brown     Hair    Brown    Eyes
    Education, Occupation and General Characteris-
    tics   Eighth Grade education.
    Home girl.  Country reared.
    American of English anc.
    _____

    Father  21          Weight 145
    Physical Build   5 Ft. 8 In.
    Drk. brown   Hair    Brown   Eyes
    Education, Occupation and General Characteris-
    tics   Eighth grade education.
    Farmer boy.  Country reared.
    American of English anc.
    _____

    Securing babies for adoption at the Nursery of The Willows, 2929 Main
    Street, Kansas City, Mo.  Either Phone 2390 South.
    Form No. 171
```

Now that Mother knew his name, she was curious to find out more about Nick. One day she asked me if I would be interested in looking for her birth father. "Sure," I said. "Let's see what I can find out about the old rounder," I said with a laugh, "but I think we need to ask Grandma Leona first."

Chapter 59

A few days later, I called Grandma Leona. I think she was prepared to hear the question when I brought up looking for Nick. I asked if she cared if I did a little research to find out more about him. I didn't want to open old wounds if she didn't want me to do so. It was enough that we had found her. Leona didn't hesitate and said she didn't care because she didn't have any connections back in that area now anyway. She said she would be interested in finding out what happened to him.

Leona told me she spent some time with Iva to recuperate body and soul after having her baby. After a couple months, they got news that Grams was sick. Leona went back home and Grams died that year. "It was one of the saddest years of my life," Leona said.

Leona stayed with her mama until she met Russell and married in 1928. They moved to Portland, Oregon, in September after Louis wrote to them about coming to work. So Leona spent a few years in Havana area after having "Marcia" but she never did see Nick. From time to time she or a family member would hear or read tidbits of information about Nick or the Belt family.

After all these many years, Leona still remembered the gal Nick married was named Velma. She also knew that Nick and Velma had a daughter that was born sometime in June 1925. So Mother had a half-sister only about four months younger than she. Leona also knew Nick and Velma had divorced. She read in the newspaper that Velma married a guy from Sedan and she remembered the last name. That was all she could recall.

This was a great place to start, and it was pretty crazy that Nick had grown up close to Sedan, Kansas, in Chautauqua County. Finding Leona May Hendrickson was from Havana and Montgomery County had been a real shock. But Sedan was even more of a surprise after spending so much time in Chautauqua County back when I worked for the Elk County Extension Service.

After my super sleuth detective work in finding Leona from Havana and all this good info on Nick, I figured this was going to be a snap. I called information to see if the last name Grandma Leona gave me for Velma was listed in Sedan. Luck was on my side as there was a listing in the phone book.

With my confidence quite high, I dialed the number and an elderly lady answered the phone. Quite honestly the "hello" was not the pleasant voice I had become accustomed to when searching for family members.

A little taken aback I said, "Ummm yes, hello, my name is KelLee Parr and I'm doing some genealogy research on my family tree. My research has led me to you and I think we might have some common ancestors. Would you have some time to answer some questions for me?"

"Well, I'm quite busy," she said rather coolly.

"Oh, okay. May I just ask if you know a Mr. Nick Virgle Belt? I think some people called him Burgie."

Velma's answered back quite sharply, "Yes, I knew a Nick Belt. I was married to him. I have nothing to say about him."

"Oh, I'm sorry to have bothered you, ma'am. Thank you for your time." And I hung up.

That short conversation shook me. I wasn't expecting that reaction but guess I should have thought through the facts and if they had divorced so quickly, things might not have been pleasant.

So this was a roadblock but hey, I actually found Nick's wife and knew she still lived in Sedan. I had been too nervous to ask about her daughter and sure wasn't about to call her again.

Chapter 60

Though I hit a little bump in the road, I wasn't about to give up looking for more information about my grandfather Nick. Mother told Leona about my conversation, or lack thereof, with Velma. I think she was as interested in finding something out about Nick as we were now. Leona sent Mother a letter and included an old, small Chautauqua County map. She had circled the little town of Monett, not too far from Sedan, and wrote:

> *Just a few lines and sending you this part of a Kansas Road Map. I circled Monett. Think Nick lived in that part of the county. I don't think you will find him alive, as he was about 2 years older than me. I don't know of anyone back there that might know him or his folks.*

Sedan, Kansas, was so familiar to me. I thought back to the years I lived in that area. My next idea was to ask some of my friends from back when I lived in neighboring Howard. None of my friends were still living there as we all "got out of Dodge" as soon as we could. However, 30 years later many of us remained the best of friends. We often vacationed together and spent many fall weekends tailgating at Kansas State University football games.

My first call was to my friend Rachelle. She was very close to my family and knew all about my quest for finding Grandma Leona. Rachelle had worked with many Extension Homemaker Units in both Elk and Chautauqua Counties, giving educational programs to the EHU ladies. I knew if she had met Velma or anyone named Belt, she would remember. Rachelle never forgot a name or phone number. We teased her that we didn't need a phone book in our Extension office, "Just ask Rachelle" was a common refrain.

Updating Rachelle about Nick and about my call to Velma, I asked if she remembered working with any of the Chautauqua County people named Belt or knew Velma. "No, I'm sorry, I don't remember working with anyone with either of those names," she said. "Have you checked with Brent or Ed? They would have a better chance of knowing them since they lived in Sedan."

"No, I haven't checked with either of them yet. They are on my list to call next."

"Well let me know what you find out. This is so exciting. I'm so happy for Wanda. Please give her my love."

"Will do. Thanks so much. Tell all your family hello for me too."

My friends, Brent and Ed, both lived and worked in Sedan when Rachelle and I lived in Howard. I decided to call Brent first.

Brent was a third grade teacher when he lived in Sedan so I figured there was a chance he might have had kids in his class with that last name. It had been a few years since Brent had taught in Sedan. He was now a teacher in Olathe, a suburb of Kansas City. He married Cindy, one of our single friends back in the Howard days. She got a job in Kansas City as a home economics extension agent and the first to escape from "Dodge."

I knew Brent and Cindy had lots of friends still living in Sedan, and they would be a good resource to possibly finding Nick. After supper I dialed their number. Brent answered and I said, "Hi, Brent. How is school going?"

"You have no idea. What a year! I will be so ready for summer break."

We chatted a little about school and our classes that year. Brent was a great teacher but for him this was the year all teachers dread: "the class from hell." He filled me in on some of the hooligans he was dealing with. I felt quite blessed my first two classes of students were so awesome.

I asked Brent how Cindy and Mikaela, their daughter, were doing. After we caught up a little, I reminded him about finding my grandmother. I shared the story with all my friends but none of them knew about my latest undertaking, searching for Nick. Quickly I filled in the details that Grandma Leona shared about Nick and about his upbringing close to Hale or Monett in Chautauqua County. I told Brent about the chilly conversation with Velma. I asked if he had heard of her but he didn't recall the name.

"I have checked with the telephone information for Sedan, but there isn't a listing with the last name of Belt. Do you remember any families from Sedan with that last name or kids that went to school in Sedan?"

"No, I never taught any kids or remember anyone with that last name," he said.

"Dang, I am hoping some of his family is still there. Grandma Leona told me about him marrying Velma, and she knew they divorced. I guess their shotgun wedding didn't last too long. Leona knew Velma married again and lived in Sedan."

"Amazing story," Brent said. "Blows me away they were all from Chautauqua and Montgomery Counties. You should ask Ed. He knew a lot more of the farming families and maybe he would have heard the name."

"Okay, thanks, I'll give him a call and see what he might know."

"You're welcome. Great to hear from you. Have a good week and tell Ed hi. We will have to get together soon this summer. Bye."

I hung up and tried calling Ed. No answer. Ed had been the county soil conservationist in Sedan and probably worked with every farmer and rancher in Chautauqua County at some point. Brent was right, if Nick Belt or any of his family were farmers, Ed would know.

When Ed left Sedan, he continued to work as a soil conservationist in Morris County in Council Grove, Kansas, until he decided to go back to K-State to get his education degree. Another teacher in our group! He was living in Manhattan at the time working on his teaching certification. Ed kept quite busy with school work and was always tough to catch at home and unfortunately this was before cell phones.

The rest of the evening I graded papers and cleaned my office. My desk was always a mess from neglect during the school year and never taking time to put things away. Running across some of Grandma Leona's letters and some photos from our last visits with her, I couldn't help but stop and feel blessed in having her in our lives. I hoped things would turn out as well if I found Nick.

Chapter 61

♡♡

Photography was one of my passions I discovered I shared with my mother. As kids growing up, all the family would tease my mother and act annoyed by her constantly taking photos or shooting movies with her movie camera and sunlight bright light. Years later my cousins, my sisters, and I appreciated her efforts and enjoyed the memories she gave us through her photos. I started to enjoy taking photos when I worked in Guatemala and had such beautiful scenery and colorful people for images to capture. Unfortunately, I wasn't as good as my mother at logging and keeping track of my photos in albums.

While in my office waiting to call Ed, I looked at all the photos of visits with Grandma Leona. It was wonderful how this had all turned out for my family. To think just a few months ago, Leona didn't even know her daughter, let alone that she had grandchildren and great-grandchildren. One of my favorite photos was Grandma Leona and her great-grandchildren, Bo and EJ, with huge smiles on their faces.

I came across a beautiful photo of an event that happened while Leona was visiting at the farm for the first time. The photo was of the beautiful, tall prairie-grass pasture across the road from the house with the sun shining brightly. It was just breaking dawn so the sun was just above the horizon and shining across the prairie. The grass colors were reds, yellows, oranges, and browns. However, there had been a rare October ice storm that night and everything was coated with a thick layer of ice. The photo was taken showing the pasture through the barbed wire fence with long icicles hanging down from the barbs. The sun was glistening off the ice and was one of the most magical sights ever at the farm.

It was so ironic to have that ice storm in October because Janice's husband, Louie, being an Alabama boy, hated the cold and snow. Jan and Louie preferred visiting the farm in the summer so Louie could fish and they seldom visited Kansas in the winter, afraid of being trapped in a snowstorm. They had thought they were safe coming in October to meet Grandma Leona. But it was like a winter wonderland. Leona loved the beauty of the Kansas prairie, even the ice, which she never saw in California. She said it reminded her of when she was a kid growing up. I thought, "It was as if God wanted to freeze this moment in time for us to always remember how special it was to have Leona in our lives."

Looking through all the photos, I hoped my good luck would continue in searching for Nick and any relatives on that side of the family. Around 9:30 p.m., I decided it was time to give Ed a call. "Hey Ed. How's it going? What's going on out in Manhattan?" I asked.

"Just super busy with classes. I'm ready to get to my student teaching. How are you? School going okay?"

"Yes, just fine. The year is going by really quickly. But I am enjoying my class. I just spoke to Brent and sounds like he is having that 'class from hell' we always dread and want to avoid."

My conversation with Ed also included our mandatory discussion of K-State sports and whatever was going on at the moment. Finally I got around to asking him what I called to ask. "Hey Ed, do you remember me telling you about finding my Grandmother Leona?"

"Oh yes, sure. That's a great story."

"Well, I was hoping maybe you or Brent might be able to help me with another piece of the puzzle," I said. "My grandmother gave us some more information about my mother's birth father."

Again I shared the news I had gleaned to date and the conversation with Velma. He didn't know her.

"When I talked to Brent earlier, he didn't remember any families or kids with the last name Belt. He suggested I talk to you since you worked with so many farmers. It turns out Nick was from a rural area northeast of Sedan. Grandma Leona thought the Belt farm was between the little communities back then called Hale and Monett. Have you ever heard of either of them?"

"Oh yeah, I remember an area northeast of Sedan that the locals called Hale. They, of course, made fun of being from "Hell." There isn't a town there anymore. But I don't remember anyone named Belt. But you know what, I think I know someone who lives in that area who would know. The Beason family lives in that area. Do you remember them?"

"Yes, I do sort of remember them coming to some of the extension farm meetings we had in Sedan or Howard."

"They're big time farmers in that area. I got to know them very well working with them over the years. They're a wonderful family and Mr. Beason's family has lived there for several generations. If anyone can help you, they can, I bet. I even think I have a Sedan phone book. Let me look up their number. Just a second."

Ed went to go look up the number. I was feeling pretty confident in calling complete strangers and asking for information until I called Velma. I hoped this lead would be more fruitful. Ed returned and gave me the number. He said, "Tell the Beasons that I gave you their names and number, and I'm sure they will be happy to help if at all possible."

"Thanks so much. I'll let you know if I have any luck."

After talking to Ed, it was time for bed and I would have to wait for another day to call the Beasons, but I had hope with this new lead.

Chapter 62

On the Saturday morning after talking to Ed, I decided it was time to call the Beasons. I dialed the number and much like my first call to Bus Wade's home, a very sweet lady's voice answered the phone. "Hello?"

"Hi, is this the Beason residence?"

"Yes, it is. May I ask who is calling?"

"My name is KelLee Parr. Ed Schmeidler is a friend of mine and he gave me your name and number to call. He said he thought you might be able to help me. I have been doing some research for my family tree and believe I have found that I might have some relation that lives or used to live in Chautauqua County."

"Well, I don't know if I can help you but would be glad to help if I can, especially if you are a friend of Ed's," she said.

"Ed and I became friends when I was the county extension agent in Elk County and he was working in the Soil Conservation Service office in Sedan," I said. "Through my research, I think I might have some relation in your area. I asked Ed if he had heard of a Nick Belt or any Belt family members. I think we might be related. Ed didn't recognize the name but said if anyone had heard of them, the Beasons probably would because your family has been in Chautauqua County for quite some time. Are you familiar with that name?" I asked.

"Oh my, yes," she said.

My heart skipped a beat. She knew the Belts!

"The farmstead where my son's house is located was the Belt farm. Many years ago my husband bought it from the Belt family. We called Nick 'Burgie.' The farm had belonged to Burgie's father, Archie. None of the Belt children wanted to farm and Burgie moved to Independence, Kansas."

"How amazing. So is Burgie still alive?" I asked.

"Oh no. He passed away quite some time ago from a heart attack, I believe. His family still lives in Independence and owns some of the land we farm today. Burgie had a sister and some of her family lives in California. They own land that we farm."

This was just getting to be way too easy. My heart pounding, I asked Mrs. Beason if she knew how I could possibly reach some of the Belt family. She told me Burgie's daughter, Suzie, lived in Independence. She was the one that they were in contact with about the farm. She gave me Suzie's phone number and address and wished me good luck in finding more information. I thanked her and sat dumbstruck after hanging up. In my hand was the address and phone number of a lady I presumed was my aunt and my mother's half-sister.

Instead of calling Suzie, I decided to give the information to my mother and let her decide how she wanted to contact her. After talking to Mrs. Beason that morning, I went out to the farm and shared with Mother the news I had found out about Nick "Burgie" and his family. She was elated to have another part of her past revealed. I shared how Ed had suggested calling the Beasons. Mrs. Beason was very nice and told me about the Belt family. I told my mother, "Mrs. Beason said Nick died of a heart attack many years ago."

Mother didn't look too surprised but a little disappointed. "Well, I suppose it was wishing for a little too much that both of them would still be alive."

"Yes, he would have been around 88 years old. Mrs. Beason told me that he had lived in Independence and has family there. The family still owns some land that the Beasons farm. She gave me the address and phone number of one of Nick's daughters named Suzie. She would be your half-sister."

Reality set in for Mother when I said she had a half-sister. She looked a little bit stunned about the fact she had more family.

"Do you want to try and reach out to Suzie and find out more?" I asked my mother.

She thought for a little bit and said, "Well, this might be a big surprise to Suzie if it was kept as big a secret as it was in Leona's family. I'd like to know more and if there are other siblings. I wonder if this is Velma's daughter or if there were other children."

"I don't know. I didn't ask Mrs. Beason or go into much detail trying to protect Leona's identity. I just said I was researching the family tree and trying to find Nick Belt."

"Well, maybe I should just write Suzie a letter rather than try and call. Say kind of what you said to Mother Leona, giving just a little information and see if she wants to reach out. What do you think?"

"I totally agree and think that's a great idea. At least with the letter, she can process the news without being put on the spot talking to you on the phone not knowing what to say."

"Okay, my heart is beating so fast," Mother said. "I can't believe you found them so easily. This is amazing. Please thank Ed for me. One more piece to the puzzle."

Chapter 63

My mother wrote a letter to Suzie in March of 1992. She explained in her letter that she had been given up for adoption when she was a baby. Just recently she discovered the identity of her birth mother and also learned that Nick Belt was her father. Mother explained how we found Nick's identity and how we found Suzie as well. She told Suzie that we had not shared with anyone, including the Beasons, the reason we were looking for Nick but just that we were doing genealogical research for our family tree.

Mother wrote:

> *This might be a total surprise if you had not known about me. I don't want to cause any disruption to you or your family's lives. I am just looking for possible family and more about their background. I will leave it up to you if you would like to contact me.*

Suzie wrote my mother back immediately and was elated to find out about her. She knew that her father had another child but didn't know any of the details. Suzie had lots of questions and asked Mother to call her. She called her that night. "Hi Suzie, I am Wanda Parr, your half-sister. Thank you for writing me back. I know this must have been quite a shock to get a letter from me."

"Oh my, yes. But I'm so happy to have found you. It was never talked about but I was told by Loyette that when Dad was young, he and a young girl had a baby. Velma made sure to tell Loyette this information. That's all Loyette was told and she never knew what happened to the other baby. I guess that's you?"

"Yes, that would be me," Mother said laughing and asked, "Now who is Loyette?"

"Loyette is my half-sister. She is Dad and Velma's daughter," Suzie shared. "Dad and Velma never got along too well. They probably should never have gotten married but you know the circumstances there. It only lasted about a year and they got a divorce. There wasn't a lot of love lost between Dad and Velma. Loyette came and lived with Dad and Mom for a while when she was young. Guess she and her mom didn't get along too well. I'm not that close to Loyette because she is quite a bit older than me, but we do keep in touch. Loyette will be 67 in June."

"That would be right. I'm 67 already. My birthday was February 14," Mother said.

"Oh my, Loyette's birthday is June 14. Exactly four months younger than you."

Suzie went on to tell her, "Dad married Mom and had us four kids, Don, Jack, Patsy (Pat) and me. Dad and Mom have both been gone quite some time. I was pretty young when Dad passed away. Don and Jack have both passed on from heart attacks, too. Pat and I both live here in Independence. Pat is 57 and she and her husband, Bill, have three grown girls, Debbie, 38, Gail, 34, and Theresa is 30. Her oldest girl, Debbie, is the same age as me."

"So you are the same age as your niece," my mother said.

Suzie laughed, "Yes, I was sort of a surprise you could say. I am 19 years younger than my sister Pat."

"My son is 36 and I have daughters 44 and 41, so you have nieces older than you," Mother added with a chuckle.

"I sure hope I get to meet you and all your family and you get to meet mine," Suzie said. "My husband's name is Lewis and I have a son Ronnie, 20, son Frank, 13, and daughter Michelle, 9."

Suzie shared that Nick's full name was Virgil Nick Belt, not spelled Virgle as Leona had written. He never liked the name

Virgil and used Nick as his legal name. He got the nickname "Burgie" when he was little and his younger brother couldn't say Virgil. It stuck and everyone always called him Burgie.

Burgie was a painter by trade and so was Suzie's brother Jack, and they occasionally worked together on jobs. Suzie shared they were both well known for their good work. She said they lived in a rock house growing up and her dad kept everything in it and around it painted as bright and shiny as a new penny. Mother could tell Suzie was very proud of her dad.

Suzie wrote to my mother shortly after they talked on the phone:

> *Dear Wanda,*
>
> *It was really nice to visit with you on the phone this morning. You can just say so much more on the phone than in a letter. I am sending an "In Remembrance" card from Dad's funeral and some pictures for you to keep.*
>
> *I just feel so sad deep inside that Dad never got to know and love you or his grandchildren. You would have loved him, too. I really do enjoy visiting with you and I've been waiting to hear from you. Write or call anytime you can. Talk to you soon. Love, Suzie*

The sisters stayed in touch and developed a wonderful relationship. Mother also got to meet her other half-sister Pat. It was quite astounding for her to know that Suzie was 29 years younger. Her father Nick had children ranging in ages from 67 to 38.

Mother shared with Leona the information about finding Nick and about talking to Suzie. She told Leona that Nick passed away from a heart attack and about his other children. Leona was sad to hear Nick had died but happy for her daughter's finding more family and answers. Mother asked Leona if she wanted to see any of the pictures that Suzie sent of Nick. Leona responded, "Only if they have a picture of him when he was younger. I really don't care to see what he looked like as an old man or his family. I would rather just remember him the way I do."

Mother was able to get a picture of her father when he was younger and shared with Leona. Leona's comment was, "Well, he was a pretty good-looking guy," and laughed.

Chapter 64

Mother asked Suzie about contacting Loyette. She wondered if Loyette would be interested in meeting her. Suzie suggested to let her call and break the news. Loyette was as surprised as Suzie, but she was excited to meet her half-sister. She called my mother and they, too, developed a friendship.

Loyette still lived in Sedan close to her mother, Velma. Mother told Loyette, "My son called and talked to Velma, asking about Nick."

Loyette laughed and said, "I bet she didn't have anything good to say if she said anything at all."

"No, he didn't get very far in the conversation. He just told her that he was doing research on the family tree and thought he might be related to Nick Belt and asked if she knew anything about him. She pretty much just said no and that was end of the conversation."

Loyette laughed. "No, my mom is pretty hard headed. Having heard both sides of the story from Mom and Dad, I know it was a good thing they divorced pretty early, or they might have shot each other. It was not a match made in heaven."

One Friday afternoon shortly after finding each other, Loyette and her husband drove three hours from Sedan to the Parr farm and spent the weekend with my parents. She brought a hand-made, porcelain doll for my mother. Loyette made the Victorian style clothes and hat herself. The doll was really beautiful and it was so sweet of her. It joined Grandma Leona's doll as one of Mother's most prized possessions.

On the Saturday Loyette and her husband were at the farm, I drove out to meet them. It was interesting just how similar my mother and Loyette were in stature and in looks as well. I shared with Loyette, "I think it is so amazing that you are from Sedan. I lived in Howard from 1984 to 1987 and worked for the extension service. We had many meetings in Sedan. I also had many friends from there and spent a lot of time visiting them there."

"Did you ever visit the Sedan Baptist Church on a Sunday morning?" she asked.

"Well, yes I did go one time with a friend. That was like seven or eight years ago."

"I knew I'd seen you before. I sat right behind you at church that day. Now isn't that amazing. Sitting right by my nephew and never even knew it. I'm sure we shook hands during the greetings."

We all laughed and realized just how small this big old world really is.

Chapter 65

Over the next several years, Wanda and her new family did a lot of writing, calling, and getting to know one another. She and Lee went to Independence to meet her sisters, Suzie and Pat. Suzie and her family also made a few trips to the farm.

One summer morning Wanda received a phone call. She answered the phone and heard a voice she didn't recognize. It was a very pleasant lady's voice with a little hint of mischievousness.

"Hello?"

"Hello, is this Wanda Parr?"

"Yes, it is. How may I help you?" Wanda asked.

"My name is Dolores Tanksley and I know you have never heard of me but I think we just might be kinfolk," Dolores chuckled and went on. "My husband is Charles Tanksley and he is a cousin to Suzie. We were just visiting recently with her and she told us about you. We were wondering if we might get to meet you."

Wanda was quite shocked but guessed it was her turn to be the one surprised by new family members. "Well, yes I would love to meet you. How is it we are related and where are you from?"

"Charles and I live in Rodeo, California," Dolores said. "We are back in Kansas visiting some family and just catching up on some business. Charles still has some family land back in Chautauqua County so we went to talk to the people who farm our land and see some of his cousins. We were visiting with Suzie and she was telling us all about you and your being Burgie's daughter. Charles' mother Mary was a sister to Burgie. So we gather that would make you and Charles first cousins," Dolores laughed.

"Oh my gosh, that is something," Wanda said. "I really hadn't thought that much about cousins. Suzie and I have only talked about immediate family."

"Well, I know this is short notice but Charles and I are in Topeka, visiting another one of his cousins. We are wondering, if you aren't too busy, if we could run out to meet you. We won't stay long. We just figured if we're this close, we should take the opportunity to meet our long lost cousin," again another chuckle from Dolores.

"Oh that would be great. We aren't going anywhere and would be so happy to meet you. It's a little ways out here to our neck of the woods. You sure you want to drive all the way out here to the farm on these old country roads? Lee, my husband, and I could drive to Topeka to meet you?" Wanda asked.

"Oh honey, no, no, we're the ones intruding on your day. We love to see the countryside and would be happy to drive out to meet you as long as I can keep Charles from getting lost," another chuckle.

"Well, I better give you good directions to find us then because I would hate to have you wandering around out here on the reservation," Wanda chuckled. "In case you get lost, stop and ask any neighbors and they'll send you our way."

"We'll send up a smoke signal if we get lost," Dolores said and they both laughed.

Wanda proceeded to give Dolores directions to the farm. They planned on Charles and Dolores arriving in the early afternoon. Lee was mowing the yard so she went to tell him that they were going to have company later. They both worked to get the yard and house ready for company, not that it took much work. Wanda figured there was just enough time to make some kolaches that would be hot and out of the oven by the time her new cousins got there. After lunch they stopped and cleaned up, waiting on their visitors to arrive.

A little after 1:00 p.m., Charles and Dolores pulled into the drive of the Flying P Farm. They were driving their big, blue Buick and it was covered with dust. Lee was sitting out in the sunroom and saw their dust stirring up on the old gravel road a good two miles from the house. He shouted to Wanda, "Looks like we have company coming."

Lee went outside to greet them while Wanda hurried to the screen door and just got outside in time to see Charles and Dolores open the huge doors on the big car. "Welcome to the Flying P," Lee's often-used quip to visitors and followed by an ornery, crooked smile that would always get an "Oh, Lee" from disgusted Wanda.

Charles and Dolores both laughed and had huge smiles on their faces. Charles was about 5'9," a little shorter than Lee's height. He had a head of white hair with a bald spot on top and big bushy white eyebrows. He had an ornery little smile like Lee's and blue eyes that gleamed with mischievousness and wisdom. "Well, thanks. It's a far ways out here. Guess I shouldn't have washed the car in Topeka to try and impress my new cousin," Charles said with a laugh.

Dolores was a stately, beautiful woman with white hair fixed up on top of her head. She had glasses almost exactly like Wanda's and a huge smile. She came around the car and headed straight for Wanda and gave her a hug. "You must be Wanda. Suzie has told us all about you and we're so happy to meet you."

Charles came up and shook Lee's hand and then gave Wanda a hug as Dolores gave Lee a hug. "It's so nice to meet you," Wanda said. "I'm sorry about your car getting so dusty. One of the pitfalls of living out in the country, but we love it here. This is the farm I grew up on."

"Well, we would've been here earlier if Charles had listened to me when I told him to turn at the corner a few miles back. He drove right on by and then we weren't sure which corner we'd missed when we came back. A nice man stopped and helped us get redirected. Said his name was Donald Miller. We told him we were going to the Parr's and he laughed and said 'You sure you want to go to see those crazy folk on the reservation?'"

"That old cuss," Lee said. "He and his wife, Ivaleu, are two of our best friends and we go on vacation with them. Heck, we even went to Jamaica with them. Never go there again."

Charles laughed and said, "Yes, Donald said you were good folk and not to be worried about losing our scalps on the reservation."

"Oh, your farm is beautiful," Dolores chimed in. "You really put a lot of work into keeping the place looking so nice. And honey, if you saw the roads we have to drive to get to our cabin in Sierra City, you wouldn't be worried about a little dust," Dolores laughed.

"Oh, thank you. I'm so glad you called. Please come in. We have so much to talk about."

Chapter 66

The rest of that summer afternoon was spent sharing and getting to know one another. They laughed and chatted as if they had known each other all their lives. Wanda showed the Tanksleys an article published in the local paper about her being adopted, her adopted Keller family and upbringing, and finding Leona. Wanda shared how Leona told her story of giving Wanda up for adoption, and about Nick being Wanda's father. Charles was able to share some of his memories of his Uncle Burgie that Wanda loved hearing.

Dolores shared she was raised in Idaho and met Charles when he was in the army during World War II. They lived in Rodeo, California, ever since they were married. They didn't have any children so it was just the two of them with many nephews and nieces. The two loved the mountains and spent a great deal of time at their family cabin in Sierra City, California, where they went for vacations in the summer and it was their next destination after leaving Kansas.

In between glasses of lemonade and eating kolaches, the summer afternoon whisked by. Charles said, "We'd better be thinking about heading out before it gets too late and can get back to town before dark. Don't want to be lost out here on the reservation."

"Where are you staying in Topeka?" Wanda asked.

Dolores chuckled and said, "Well, we spent the night at a pretty crummy motel 'cause Charlie here's so cheap. We already visited cousin Alma yesterday in Topeka so we checked out of the motel this morning. We just figured we would either go back to Topeka tonight or start on west heading to California and maybe stop in Manhattan or Salina, depending on how tired we are. We retired folk don't have any real schedule."

"Well, if you're in no hurry, why don't you just spend the night here," Wanda offered. "We've just started getting to know you and we have a spare bedroom."

"We can't impose on you like that. Heck, we've already taken up your whole afternoon," Charles said.

"Oh no, not at all. This is wonderful having you here. You can just spend the night and I'll fix supper. Do you like to play cards?" Wanda asked.

Dolores about fell out of her chair laughing. "Do we like to play cards? We love to play cards!"

"Well, it's settled then," Lee said. "Dolores and I officially take you two cousins on and we'll kick your butts. What's the game of choice?"

It turned out that the two couples just hit it off. Anyone who didn't know them would have figured they were lifelong friends. They played dominoes, pitch, and a new game called "Hand and Foot" that the Tanksleys taught Lee and Wanda. They had such a grand time that the little "meet and greet" turned into a three-day, two-night visit.

Lee took Charles around to see the farm and cattle. Dolores and Wanda looked at tons of old photos. Dolores gave more insight into Charles' family and Wanda soaked up every word. She also was amazed to find out how many similarities she and Charles had. Dolores picked up on it pretty quickly. They both were fix-it kind of people and both a little hard headed. Dolores chuckled the laugh that Wanda came to love and said, "That hard headedness, like you telling us we're staying the night and nothing we could say about it. That is something you and Charles have in common and is definitely a 'Belt' trait."

Wanda laughed and added, "And from what Mother Leona says, a Hendrickson trait too."

The visit was wonderful and a very strong and steadfast friendship formed. Charles and Dolores kept in touch after getting home to California. Another California phone number was dialed on a regular basis. When Lee and Wanda decided to go visit Leona, they were invited to go to Charles and Dolores' first before they flew on to visit Leona.

Charles and Dolores made it back the next year to the farm and spent a week with Lee and Wanda. They had a great time going to the Prairie Band Casino just a few miles east of the farm. Turned out none of them were much of gamblers and they would rather go home and play cards, which they did every night and often during the day while visiting. During this visit, Charles and Dolores also were able to meet the rest of Wanda's brothers and sisters. Just as Leona was welcomed with open arms as part of the Keller family, so were Charles and Dolores.

While Charles and Dolores were staying at the farm, Jane called and suggested they all should come to Florida and stay at her house. The foursome quickly decided they needed some Florida sunshine the coming winter. They packed their bags and flew to Jacksonville, where they spent a week together with Jane at the beach and, of course, played cards. The highlight of the trip was their jaunt to St. Augustine and seeing the old fort. Of course, Dolores was determined to see the Fountain of Youth and get a drink.

Chapter 67

♡♡

Lee and Wanda loved to travel and vacationed with several other couples including the Sages, Millers, and Dodges. They traveled all around the country over the years and there was no doubt they had a good time. One trip they went on with the Dodges was a bus trip sponsored by a Topeka radio station. The early morning radio talk show hosts had been the tour guides on the trip. Needless to say, we weren't too surprised when the hosts upon returning home said on their first radio morning show broadcast, "We had a great time on this trip and what a fantastic group this year. We especially want to thank the Parrs and Dodges for making this trip so much fun."

The Tanksleys now were added to Lee and Wanda's list of traveling companions. Three years after the trip to Florida, Dolores called Wanda out of the blue on a cold January day and said "Get your bags packed, girl, we are going to Calgary."

Sometime during one of their conversations, Lee mentioned how he loved rodeos and always wanted to go to the Calgary Stampede in Canada. Charles and Dolores decided they wanted to make this happen for him so they planned the whole trip, made reservations for the Stampede, and motel reservations. They called Lee and Wanda to tell them they were sending tickets to fly to California and taking them to the Stampede. This trip to Canada was just another opportunity to travel and Lee and Wanda didn't even hesitate to say "yes."

In July of 1995, Lee and Wanda flew to the Tanksleys in California, and they drove to the cabin Charles and Dolores built together near Sierra City, California. They loved their beautiful cabin and spent many summer days there with family and friends. Charles and Dolores were so happy to get to share their remote retreat with their cousins. As they climbed the steep, gravel road up the mountain to reach the cabin, Wanda understood Dolores' comment the first day they met at the Flying P Farm and how a little Kansas dust on their car was nothing.

The friends spent a few days in the mountains of California playing cards and enjoying the cool summer days. Heading north, they stopped in Idaho to see where Dolores was raised and meet some of her family. With reservations in hand, they made it to Calgary. The Calgary Stampede, billed as the world's richest tournament-style rodeo, lasts for almost two weeks each July. Dolores bought tickets for several nights of the rodeo. Of course, Lee's favorite event was the chuckwagon races. The smile on Lee's face the entire three days they were there was precious, and they all had an incredible time. What more could you ask for— good food, fantastic rodeo, and playing cards with great friends.

One afternoon they all were tired and decided they needed to rest a bit. They went to their motel rooms and took a little nap. Wanda woke up and realized Lee was not in the room. She looked outside and there was no sign of him. While on the trip, Charles, Dolores and Wanda had noticed that Lee seemed to have a few issues with remembering things and repeating himself. One thing they thought might have been the cause was Lee ran out of the nitroglycerin patches he wore every day for some heart problems. Without them he was a little lethargic and forgetful. They were finally able to get some patches at a pharmacy after going a day or two without them. It helped when Lee got them, but when he turned up missing, Wanda panicked.

She knocked on Charles and Dolores's door. Charles came to the door. "Have you seen Lee?" Wanda asked. "He's gone."

"No, I haven't seen him. I just woke up and Dolores is gone too. Maybe the two of them went for a walk."

Charles and Wanda headed out and heard some music coming from the street corner a couple blocks away from the motel. They decided to go that way in their search for the two wanderers. As they got closer, they could see a crowd of people filling up the street. To their amazement as they reached the source of the music, they found a country western band with nearly a hundred people enjoying the music and watching square dancers out in the street. Wouldn't you know, Dolores and Lee were out in the middle of the crowd do-si-doing. Nobody would ever have thought the two of them (both had bum knees and had been limping around all week) would be out dancing. But there they were, having a grand ol' time!

What an amazing bond developed between the two cousins and their spouses. Cousins, who until just a few years prior, didn't even know the other existed As the stay in Calgary ended, the four headed out of Canada and back to California with one final stop along the way. Dolores told Wanda she and Charles would like to meet Leona if that would be okay. Wanda wondered how her mother would feel meeting Nick's nephew and asked Leona, saying it was okay if she wasn't comfortable with it. Leona said, "I'd be happy to meet them, especially if it means getting to see you and Lee."

So the four made the long trek from Calgary to Klamath Falls, Oregon, and finally to Dorris, California, to visit Leona. Wanda knew that Leona would love Charles and Dolores but was still a little nervous as they walked up to knock on the door. Wanda noticed the two little handmade wooden decorations hanging from the porch rafters of a little girl and boy on old swings. She had sent those to Leona the previous Mother's Day.

Wanda's anxiousness was unwarranted and after hugs and greetings, Dolores gave Leona one of her handmade afghans, and Leona beamed with appreciation that she made it for her. She proudly placed the afghan on the back of the couch for all to see. Leona was so happy to see Wanda and Lee. It had been almost a year since they last got together when Leona and her niece Darlene went back to Kansas. Charles and Dolores fit right in and the conversation quickly began to flow.

While sitting in the comfy living room, Wanda smiled as she looked at the beautiful brick fireplace that covered the south wall. The mantel that ran the entire distance was filled with new photos that were missing from the first visit a few years before. Now next to photos of Darlene's and Orville's families were photos of her new family. Leona proudly displayed her daughter and son-in-law's photo front and center. The once partially filled mantel was now lined with photos of her grandchildren and great-grandchildren. How it warmed Wanda's heart to know Leona was proud to show the world her secret.

The four shared about their great trip to Calgary. Lee told about the chuckwagon races and how it reminded him of the chariot races Orville took them to on their last visit to Leona's. Charles and Leona swapped wonderful memories of growing up in southeast Kansas. Leona brought out her pineapple upside-down cake, and they all made over how good it was.

While they sat at the dining room table and shared more about their Canadian journey, Leona was thinking about the truly incredible journey she had made since the day she received a random letter asking her about the secret she had kept for so many years.

Now in her home sat her loving daughter, whom until recently was just a sad memory from a time long ago, and her son-in-law, who she came to adore and was so proud to have married her daughter. And there, across from her was Nick's nephew Charles and his wife. Charles looked so much like what Leona would expect Nick to look like at that age. So strange how life can come round full circle. As Charles shared the story of the first time meeting Dolores, Leona thought back to that first time she met Nick, the most handsome man at the dance. Her first love and the cause of so much pain in her life but now so much joy. Looking at Charles, Leona felt a pang of sadness for Nick that he never got to know his daughter.

Reflecting back to her long-kept secret now totally exposed and looking at her beautiful daughter, Leona smiled. She held in her hand the gold heart from her necklace she never took off, "Together we are complete." She wished her husband, Russell, and her brother, Louis, could have known Wanda. They would have loved her as much as she did. All those years of sad tears were replaced with happy tears and they rolled down her cheek as she realized her life was complete. "I have my Marcia, my little Valentine, for the rest of my life."

KelLee is a native Kansan. He loves his country roots and the blessing of having a wonderful family and great friends. He has enjoyed many different careers including being an agriculture missionary in Guatemala, county extension ag and 4-H agent, third grade teacher, adjunct professor and editor and project manager in writing elementary science curriculum. KelLee is a proud graduate of Kansas State University and resides in Manhattan, Kansas. He enjoys the beauty of the Flint Hills and is an ardent fan of K-State football and basketball.

Made in the USA
Columbia, SC
14 August 2017